SPEEDWAY PUBLIC LIBRARY
3 5550 43029 4952

P9-BZY-732

WITHDRAWN
Speedway Public Library

GREAT EVENTS OF THE 20th CENTURY

Published by TIME Books
Time Inc., 1271 Avenue of the Americas, New York, NY 10020
Library of Congress Catalog Card Number: 97-60987
ISBN #1-883013-15-1

Printed in the United States of America.

TIME

GREAT EVENTS OF THE 20th CENTURY

By the Editors of TIME

GREAT EVENTS of

ESSAY

NATIONS

BUSINESS

DISASTERS

JULY 4, 1986 **The 20th Century celebrates the restoration of a prominent icon from the 19th century, the Statue of Liberty**

the 20th CENTURY

SOCIETY

DISCOVERIES

SCIENCE

SPORT

THE ARTS

TIME

TIME MAGAZINE

Managing Editor: Walter Isaacson
President: E. Bruce Hallett
Publisher: Jack Haire
Consumer Marketing Director: Kenneth Godshall

GREAT EVENTS OF THE 20TH CENTURY

Editor: Kelly Knauer
Art Director: Gigi Fava
Research Director: Leah Gordon
Picture Editor: Rose Keyser
Production Editor: Michael Skinner
Copydesk: Bruce Christopher Carr, Ellin Martens, Robert Braine
Art Associate: Steve Conley
Research Associates: Anne Hopkins, Valerie Marchant

TIME INC. HOME ENTERTAINMENT

Managing Director: David Gitow
Director, Continuities and Single Sales: David Arfine
Director, Continuities: Michael Barrett
Assistant Director, Continuities: John Sandklev
Product Managers: Robert Fox, Michael Holahan, Amy Jacobsson, Jennifer McLyman
Manager, Retail and New Markets: Tom Mifsud
Associate Product Managers: Alison Ehrmann, Dan Melore, Pamela Paul, Charlotte Siddiqui, Allison Weiss, Dawn Weland
Assistant Product Managers: Alyse Daberko, Meredith Shelley, Betty Su
Editorial Operations Manager: John Calvano
Fulfillment Director: Michelle Gudema
Financial Manager: Tricia Griffin
Assistant Financial Manager: Heather Lynds
Marketing Assistant: Lyndsay Jenks

CONSUMER MARKETING DIVISION

Production Director: John E. Tighe
Book Production Manager: Donna Miano-Ferrara
Assistant Book Production Manager: Jessica McGrath

Thanks to: Ames Adamson, Ken Baierlein, Robin Bierstedt, Andrew Blau, Richard Duncan, Linda Freeman, Marti Golon, Arthur Hochstein, Ed Jamieson, Susan Langholz, Amy Musher, Rudi Papiri, Ron Plyman, Anthony Ross, Barrett Seaman, Michele Stephenson, Cornelis Verwaal, Miriam Winocur, Beth Zarcone, Carrie Zimmerman

FOREWORD

THIS BOOK IS AN ANTHOLOGY OF THE MOST SIGNIFICANT EVENTS OF the 20th century, as reported by TIME magazine. In organizing the book, we have categorized these key events of the century just as TIME treats the key events of the week: by classifying them under the familiar headings of national news, business news, society news and so on. Because so many of the events that the weekly magazine would categorize as "Nation" stories overlap with events that would be classified as "World" stories, we have combined these two sections into a single editorial area called Nations.

Many of the stories include verbatim selections from original TIME issues, appearing in sidebars. Much of the main text is also drawn from TIME's original reporting, with the material reworked, updated and researched again for historical accuracy. Even major events that occurred before TIME began publication in 1923—such as the Bolshevik revolution in Russia or the Treaty of Versailles—have proved so important to subsequent history that they have been extensively treated by TIME over the years, providing ample material for this volume.

The introductory essay, "Reveille for a Century," is based on an essay that ran in TIME's Jan. 2, 1950, Man of the Year issue. The editors prefaced their selection of Winston Churchill as "Man of the Half-Century" with an essay that provided a tour of the horizon at the dawn of the 20th century, and an update of that piece from our perspective near the end of the century seemed the ideal overture for this book.

No doubt many readers will find themselves disagreeing with our selection of the century's great events. But we suspect that part of the pleasure of this kind of volume is that it invites readers to take a mental stroll through the century and compile their own personal album of its most significant moments—with special attention to those we failed to include!

Kelly Knauer

REVEILLE

for a CENTURY

TIMES SQUARE, 1900.

Horatio Alger, his rags-to-riches message in popular bloom, had died the year before. Stephen Crane, who had seen more of the rags than the riches and had written the brutally naturalistic novel *Maggie: A Girl of the Streets*, would die shortly at 28. Pessimism and doubt were not hard to find on January 1, 1900, but the world, and especially the U.S., sided with the optimistic Alger. It looked forward to the 20th century with a degree of confidence unequaled by any previous age and unregained since. Paced fast or slow, progress was sure, limitless, irreversible. Virtue walked with progress, they fed each other.

In New York City, which was to become the symbol and the power focus of the new century, the weather on New Year's Day struck just the right note. "The snowflakes," said the approving *Times*, "were of that fine, crisp quality that lie flat and wear well." The snow, the prosperity of the land and the mood of the hour seemed to wipe out the black misery of preceding centuries. The worst was over; man was out of the woods.

The year that opened with the glitter of snow and hope was to be relatively quiet—a year of intermission between the first and second acts of a great drama. Since 1848 certain fateful ideas and forces had been gathering momentum. Nationalism,

Darwinism, socialism, secularism were all clearly recognizable by 1900. Afterward, in the second act, they were to combine and explode. In 1900 all knew that change was in the air, but it was to be gradual and upward, in accordance with popular conceptions of what Mr. Darwin's comforting theory of evolution meant in terms of human society. Few suspected the chasms ahead. Yet as 1900 unfolded, there were portents.

WORKERS, ARISE!

IN GERMANY A BURNING, BITTER, SARDONIC 30-year-old Russian exile, **V.I. Lenin,** was preparing the premier issue of his paper *Iskra* (The Spark), which was designed to quicken the class struggle in Russia. That first issue dedicated *Iskra* to training "people who will devote to the revolution not only their spare evenings but the whole of their lives." No periodical ever adhered more closely and successfully to its prospectus.

In South Africa another revolutionary, Mohandas Gandhi, 31, organized an ambulance corps of Indians to help the British in the Boer War. Gandhi was an idealistic lawyer who had emigrated from one outpost of the British Empire, his native India, to another, South Africa. His personal sympathies were with the Boers, but he reasoned that he must stand by the British because progress for Indians could come only within the empire.

In China the Boxers rebelled. They were swept aside, but the cause of Chinese self-determination would be taken up by the son of a peasant in the province of Hunan who was only seven years old in 1900. Forty-nine years later, Mao Zedong's Marxist guerrillas would conclude a lengthy civil war by entering Beijing in triumph.

In Kaiser Wilhelm's Germany, Prince Von Bülow had told the Reichstag three weeks before the new year, "In the coming century Germany will be either the hammer or the anvil." Adolf Hitler, an 11-year-old Austrian schoolboy in 1900, would emerge after Germany's bitter defeat in World War I to lead the nation to both of Von Bülow's destinies. Hitler forged an unbroken series of diplomatic and military conquests, but the legacies of his Reich were the Götterdämmerung of a ruined Berlin, a divided Germany and the unspeakable horrors of the Holocaust.

The career of Hitler was the proof that progress can be both poison and elixir, that evil is ineradicable and that safety is the most foolish of all foolish human hopes.

CENTER OF THE UNIVERSE

THE WORLDS OF HITLER AND GANDHI, MAO and Lenin seemed far apart in 1900. Yet however diverse their perspectives, they converged in a common focus: Britain, the banker, educator and policeman to the world. And the focus had a symbol, **Victoria Regina.** On the throne since 1837—long before the memory of most living men and women—she embodied sureness, security, principle. After her husband Prince Albert died in 1861, she had his evening clothes laid out every night as a memorial ritual of constancy. She once rebuked a minister who used the word expediency: "My lord, I have been taught to judge between what was right and what was wrong; 'expediency' is a word I neither wish to hear again nor to understand."

On the night of May 17, 1900, Victoria rejoiced. Her troops that day had relieved Mafeking, besieged seven months by the rebellious Boers. Though no great war, this had been the gravest challenge to Pax Britannica since Waterloo, four years before Victoria was born. On Mafeking night at Windsor Castle, Eton boys sang patriotic songs for the old Queen. She sat by a window in the dusk; the Eton boys were delighted when an Indian servant handed the Queen a whiskey and soda, which she drank, along with all Britain, on Mafeking night.

Months later, on January 22, 1901, Victoria died in the arms of her grandson, Kaiser Wilhelm, whose devotion to her was widely advertised. Yet in a secret message to the Czar, the Kaiser had recently made an offer: if the Czar would send his armies against India, the Kaiser would guarantee that no European nation rose to Britain's defense. The world of Windsor Castle was not as secure as it seemed on Mafeking night.

INVENTING THE FUTURE

THE FORCES THAT WOULD UPSET VICTORIAN equilibrium were not political alone. Science and commerce, even the arts, would tear down old certainties and create increasingly complex models of nature and man. Even as Victoria's death drew the curtain across the 19th century, many of the most definitive catalysts of change in the new century were taking their place on the stage.

In garages in both Europe and America, inventors were tinkering with the newfangled horseless carriage. **Henry Ford,** 37 in 1900, was one of them. He had built his first automobile in 1896; in 1899 he resigned from his job at the Edison Illuminating Company in Detroit to concentrate on improving his vehicles. In 1908 he unveiled his Model T, the first car common people could afford. His "Tin Lizzie" sparked a social revolution that has yet to end.

In 1900, at Kitty Hawk in North Carolina, two shade-tree mechanics from Ohio, Orville and Wilbur Wright, were flying kitelike gliders, which led them in three years' time to the first powered flight of a heavier-than-air machine. It took some years for the world to realize that this ingenious toy had revolutionized war and peace.

As the century turned, communications also were speeding up. The telephone was already an established fact of life in major cities. Now, in 1901, Guglielmo Marconi, 26, succeeded in sending a radio signal across the Atlantic. By 1920 broadcasting entrepreneurs such as David Sarnoff dreamed of placing a radio on every kitchen table—and when they succeeded, they began to dream of placing a television in every living room. A novel dynamic was born: revenues from new media funded new technologies. So radio gave way to TV, the Victrola to the long-playing record, the LP to the compact disc.

A MALLEABLE COSMOS

EVEN AS FORD, MARCONI AND THE WRIGHTS were putting liberating new tools into men's hands, theoretical physicists were redrafting our view of the most basic laws of time and energy, light and motion. To the grave, sedate scientists of the late 19th century, the physical world seemed as orderly as one of Queen Victoria's garden parties. Its byways held a few shadows still, but these most scientists were sure would soon be lightened. But in the neatly appropriate year of 1900, a discovery was made that was to knock the props from under classical physics. In his Berlin laboratory, Max Planck, a 42-year-old German physicist, discovered that atoms emit and absorb radiant energy in sudden invisible bursts—quanta—rather than in a continuous flow, and that energy could be defined in terms of its relationship to matter.

A second revolution came in 1905: **Albert Einstein,** a young patent examiner, published four papers that redrafted the basic physical laws of the universe. The most important of them introduced the notion of relativity, suggesting that time and space were not constant but malleable—and suddenly the very ground beneath men's feet seemed less firm.

As particle physicists began to smash the supposedly indivisible atom to reveal the mysterious forces within, science receded further from the grasp of the average man. In 1945 U.S. atomic scientists harnessed Einstein's revelations to create the devastating atom bomb, and the shock waves of Hiroshima and Nagasaki forever shattered the notion that scientific progress walked with virtue.

SOUNDING INTERIOR DEPTHS

IN THE NEW CENTURY'S FIRST YEARS, WHILE Einstein was unveiling a new model of the cosmos, Sigmund Freud, 44, a Viennese neurologist, was opening new pathways into man's unconscious mind. In mid-career, Freud at the turn of the century was just beginning to achieve worldwide notoriety for his theories. With the 1899 publication of *The Interpretation of Dreams* and the 1905 appearance of *Three Essays on the Theory of Sexuality,* Freud began an exploration of man's innermost realms as significant as the discoveries of the new physics.

The ferment that was bubbling under the surface of the new century could only be captured by equally radical new forms of art. In the fine arts, the chief standard-bearer of change was **Pablo Picasso.** As if on cue, the 19-year-old Picasso arrived in Paris from Spain in 1900 to begin his life's work. At first he emulated others, but by 1907 he would break through to a new form of expression in *Les Demoiselles d'Avignon,* a sneak preview of the future that shocked viewers with its brute power. Working with Georges Braque, Picasso went on to develop Cubism, which eerily mirrored in paint Einstein's shifting, complex perspectives of time and space.

In 1900 James Joyce, who would create equally revolutionary forms in literature, was studying at Dublin's Catholic University; four years later he would leave his native land to forge a new style, untainted by Ireland's antique mores. Artists of this new century would seek to challenge and confront; they would be outsiders, whether their exile was voluntary, like Joyce's, or involuntary, like that of Mann and Brecht, Solzhenitsyn and Rushdie.

MAKING THE NEWS NEW

NEW FORMS OF ENERGY AND NEW MEANS OF motion, the rise of the mass market, the exploration of the unconscious mind, the beacon of revolutionary Marxism—the seeds of the coming century were taking root even as the Empress of the old order toasted victory at Mafeking. Soon they would blossom, some into flowers so evil they might have challenged even Stephen Crane's pessimism, some into miracles so beneficial they might have stymied even Horatio Alger's optimism.

The magazine that would most completely chronicle the century's changes—TIME—would not be born until 1923. In 1900 TIME's co-founder, **Henry Luce,** was a two-year-old in Tengchow, China, the son of Presbyterian missionaries. As much a maker of new forms as Ford or Picasso, Luce designed TIME to deliver the news to busy people in a highly compressed, accelerated fashion that matched the pulse of the times.

Through eight decades TIME has written the story of the period Luce christened the American Century. When Luce coined this term in a 1941 LIFE essay, many scorned it as boosterish and boastful. Yet as the century ends, with the U.S. the world's sole superpower, with democracy and capitalism ascendant even in the former strongholds of communism, with world culture scrambling to keep up with the digital dazzle of ever changing Times Square, Luce's term can be seen as historically accurate. In these pages we revisit some of the most memorable stories TIME has covered in Luce's American Century. ■

TIMES SQUARE 1997

FIDEL CASTRO
JANUARY 26, 1959

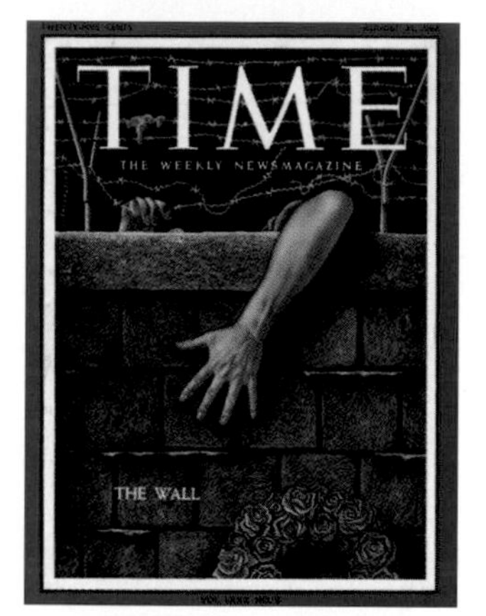

THE BERLIN WALL
AUGUST 31, 1962

AYATULLAH KHOMEINI
AUGUST 17, 1987

REFRACTED THROUGH THE infallible lens of hindsight, the great motifs of 20th century politics are clear. At the century's dawn, one superpower—Britain—dominated world affairs; at its end, another superpower—America—played the same role. But the passing of the torch demanded blood and toil, tears and sweat. It demanded two world wars, the second of them a desperate but triumphant crusade against fascist dictatorship. It demanded the steely nerve to win a new kind of war, a cold war, in the century's longest conflict, the struggle between communism and democracy. And it demanded vision: the vision that freed former colonies, formed alliances, founded new nations, funded the Marshall Plan and, finally, brought the bricks of the Berlin Wall crashing down.

NATIONS

"As the 20th Century plunged on, long-familiar bearings were lost in the mists of change. Winston Churchill's chief contribution was to warn of rocks ahead, and to launch the lifeboats. That the free world survived was due in large measure to his exertions."

–TIME, JANUARY 2, 1950

20th century

JANUARY 2, 1950

HALF-CENTURY SUPPLEMENT
★ ★ ★ WITH 4 PAGES OF COLOR MAPS ★ ★ ★

TIME

THE WEEKLY NEWSMAGAZINE

MAN OF THE HALF-CENTURY
He launched the lifeboats.

VOL. LV NO. 1

ELEGY FOR AN EMPIRE

JANUARY 22, 1901: QUEEN VICTORIA DIES

At her death, Queen Victoria, Empress of India, was so elderly only her oldest subjects could remember a time when she did not sit upon the British throne, presiding over an empire so vast the sun never set upon it. Victoria had reigned since 1837; born four years after the Battle of Waterloo, she died two years before the first airplane flight.

Seldom does history drop such a convenient curtain on the end of an era. When 82-year-old Victoria died at the dawn of the new century, the British Empire was the greatest political power on earth, sustained by its mighty navy, and a Pax Britannica prevailed from Sidney to Saskatchewan, the Seychelles to the Falklands—with the glaring exception of South Africa, where militant Dutch settlers, the Boers, were fighting for autonomy from British rule.

1901 Artist's version of McKinley's shooting

Britain's empire survived Victoria's death: it would take two world wars and decades of unrest in the colonies before the Union Jacks began to be hauled down on flagstaffs around the globe. Britons remember the **Edwardian Age,** after Victoria's death and before World War I, as the last hurrah of imperial pomp and circumstance.

Across the Atlantic, America was hurled into the 20th century as swiftly as Britain. On September 6, 1901, President **William McKinley** was fatally shot in Buffalo, New York, and his dynamic Vice President, **Theodore Roosevelt,** 42, was sworn in to succeed him. Roosevelt was the archetype of a new era: a trust-busting, rough-riding, big-stick-toting energy machine, determined to haul America into a new age. In these two transfers of power—the passing of an elderly Empress in Britain and the ascendance of a vigorous young leader in America—the narrative arc of the century was foreshadowed in its first year. ■

RUE, BRITANNIA
Victoria's son and heir, King Edward VII, 59, follows the caisson bearing her coffin

Holding portraits of the Czar, Russian workers march for reforms

REVOLT AGAINST THE OLD ORDER

JANUARY 9, 1905: REBELLION IN RUSSIA

So earth-shaking was Russia's great Bolshevik revolution of 1917 that history often forgets that the first fissures in the great empire of the Czars appeared 12 years before. On "Bloody Sunday" in the first month of 1905, 300,000 of Czar Nicholas II's subjects marched on his Winter Palace in St. Petersburg to demand reforms, including a representative assembly and an eight-hour workday.

Though the protesters bore aloft pictures of their "Little Father" to demonstrate fealty to the Czar, he rejected their petition and sent his troops against them. The soldiers opened fire, more than 100 people were killed, and the country erupted into outright rebellion. Communist firebrands like Vladimir Ulyanov—a.k.a. **Lenin**—pounced upon the tragedy to rally support. Peasants rioted, workers struck, universities were in turmoil, and sailors on board the battleship ***Potemkin*** mutinied. Meanwhile, the Czar's army and navy were being routed by the Japanese in the **Russo-Japanese War.** In October, Nicholas II was forced to issue a manifesto agreeing to the formation of a parliamentary body, the Duma, and granting the vote—as well as freedom of speech, assembly and association—to his people.

1901 Canadians storm a Boer fortress

Everywhere, old empires were in turmoil. South Africa was still reeling from the **Boer War** between Dutch settlers and the British. In China **Dr. Sun Yat-sen's** rebels toppled the world's most ancient monarchy in less than a year. In Japan victory over the Russians fueled the ascendance of the generals; in a few decades they would lead their Emperor into disaster.

In July 1908 the vast Ottoman Empire was shaken when the **Young Turks** revolted, and soon its Adriatic and Balkan provinces were up in arms. It was here, in "Balkanized" Sarajevo, that the shot that set off World War I would be fired. ■

"At Peking, Death won its inevitable victory. Its victim was Dr. Sun Yat-sen, founder and leader of the Kuo Mintang (Young China) Party. Sun was born in a small village near Canton, where the people are the "old" Chinese. As a boy, he traveled far to reside with his brother, a prosperous contractor, at Honolulu. There the spark of revolt against the lethargic and superstitious regime of the Son of Heaven was ignited... In 1911, the revolution unfurled its desperate banners; and, by the 12th day of the following year, China, the oldest of monarchies, had become a republic."

—TIME, MARCH 23, 1925

DR. SUN YAT-SEN
With Chiang Kai-shek, 1912

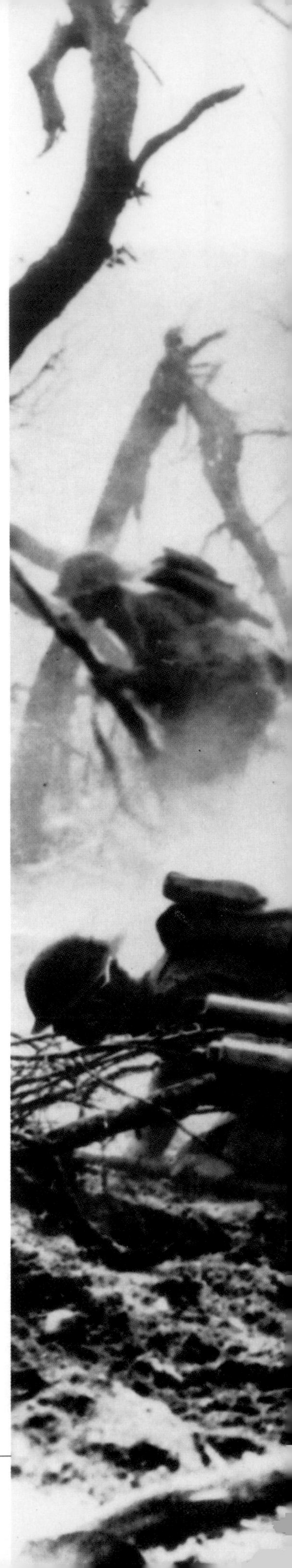

MASSACRE OF THE INNOCENTS

AUGUST 1914: WORLD WAR I BEGINS

On June 28, a Serb nationalist in obscure Sarajevo in the Balkans assassinated Archduke Franz Ferdinand of Austria-Hungary; it was the spark that touched off the first of the century's two great wars. Bound by the chains of interlocking alliances, goaded by a military that had binged on a buildup of massive battleships, governments around the world sent their sons marching off to battle, or, more accurately, to certain slaughter.

1914 Archduke Ferdinand, moments before his death

When a German drive on Paris bogged down near the Marne River in September, the troops dug in, and a new kind of warfare began—a static stalemate between trench-bound armies, punctuated by mass killings waged over a few yards of land.

The two alliances—Austria-Hungary, Germany and Turkey on the one side; England, France and Russia on the other—fought one battle after another to inconclusive ends, at an incalculable cost. At **Ypres,** at **Verdun,** at the **Somme,** a generation of young European men marched into the guns and were mowed down in droves. Progress in this war came only in the technology of killing: for the first time airplanes, submarines and tanks were used as weapons, and early in 1915 the Germans unleashed a horrific new agent of death, poison gas.

At first the U.S. was smugly isolationist. But America was drawn into the war by German submarine attacks on commercial ships at sea—like the big British liner ***Lusitania,*** which went down in 1915 with 128 Americans aboard. After a German plot to entice Mexico into an anti-U.S. alliance was discovered, Congress declared war in April 1917. By the spring of 1918, 4 million fresh U.S. troops were "over there," and their impact helped bring the exhausted German side to the peace table. ■

THE SPOILS OF WAR
U.S. troops of the 22nd Infantry, 2nd Division, fighting in the Argonne woods in France, 1918

SHORTCUT TO REVOLUTION

NOVEMBER 7, 1917: THE RUSSIAN REVOLUTION In the third year of World War I, Russia was in tatters. Battered by German triumphs, disheartened by bread riots and other signs of popular hostility, Czar Nicholas II abdicated in March 1917 and handed over power to a provisional government. Into this crucible of chaos the Germans hurled the agent who would finally destabilize their enemy to the East: Marxist rebel Vladimir Ulyanov—**Lenin.** Like a dread disease, he passed from Switzerland through Germany on a closed train, arriving at the Finland station in Petrograd (formerly St. Petersburg) on April 16, 1917. He quickly marshaled his growing cadre of communists, the **Bolsheviks,** in hopes of taking power.

When renewed rioting broke out in July, Prince Georgi Y. Lvov, the head of the czar's provisional government, banned the Bolsheviks, sent Lenin into hiding and arrested his fellow revolutionary leader, **Leon Trotsky.** Lvov then resigned, handing the reins to his War Minister, **Alexander Kerensky,** who called in troops to maintain order in Petrograd, Russia's capital.

By fall, Trotsky was out of jail again. He mobilized a fighting force of Red Guards—but the government troops would not fight them. In the vacuum of power, Lenin called for an armed uprising. Almost without opposition, the Bolsheviks seized government buildings, electric plants and finally the Winter Palace, where Kerensky's Cabinet had taken refuge.

By 1918 Lenin had banned all other political parties in Russia. By 1921 he had defeated the last remnants of resistance, the "White" armies. His Union of Soviet Socialist Republics was now the standard bearer for the worldwide Marxist revolution, and its conflict with the democracies of the West would shape the century. ■

RISE UP! Lenin in full cry, with Trotsky at right

TURNCOATS These imperial troops joined the Bolshevik cause in Petrograd

NATIONS

ARCHITECTS OF DISASTER

JUNE 28, 1919: THE TREATY OF VERSAILLES

When the German delegation of 180 diplomats and technicians went to Versailles in 1919 to negotiate the peace treaty ending World War I, the French forced their train to creep along at 10 m.p.h. so that the Germans would absorb a vivid reminder of the ruination their armies had wrought. The journey foreshadowed the treaty that was to come, for the Allied terms the Germans accepted at Versailles were harsh monuments to vengeance.

1918 Late in the war, the first tanks appeared in battle

The terms, primarily championed by France's Premier **Georges Clemenceau:** Germany would give up vast lands to France on its west and to Poland on its east and north. The Austro-Hungarian and Turkish empires would be chopped up into a goulash of new nations like Czechoslovakia and Yugoslavia. Germany alone would be forbidden to maintain more than 100,000 troops—and no warships, submarines, warplanes or tanks. The Germans would have to admit to being guilty of aggression and would pay for all war damages, an immense sum. **Winston Churchill,** one observer with foresight, knew that the treaty would breed a thirst for revenge in the proud Germans: he called it "malignant and silly."

Germany was in a state of turmoil, ruin and mass hunger. It had lost nearly 2 million men, its mutinous army had all but disintegrated, and **Kaiser Wilhelm II** had fled into exile. So the Germans signed—and disaster followed. When they stalled in paying their reparations in 1923, the French seized their industrial Ruhr Valley. As hyperinflation ravaged Germany, resentment and revenge took root in the hearts of the defeated, including that of **Adolf Hitler.** Twenty-one years later, he would stand victorious in Paris—and order the master copy of the treaty burned. ■

THE HALL OF MIRRORS
The small-minded treaty was signed in Louis XIV's oversize palace outside Paris

The League of Nations

Even before he arrived in Europe to attend the peace conference following World War I, the idealistic American president, Woodrow Wilson, issued a set of guidelines for a new world order he described as the "14 Points." Grumbled France's Premier Clemenceau: "Ten commandments were enough

WOODROW WILSON *was a failed apostle of global unity*

for God almighty!" Wilson's final point called for the creation of an international body—The League of Nations—that would act as arbiter and peacemaker in national disputes. It was a tough sell, yet he persuaded the Allies to back the League. But Wilson failed to sell the League to a U.S. Congress and people only too eager to retreat from the international arena into America's traditional isolationism. Wilson argued the merits of the League on a nationwide tour, but he suffered a pair of strokes while traveling that left him an invalid for the rest of his term. The U.S. never joined Wilson's idealistic international body.

NATIONS

HARD TIMES

MARCH 4, 1932: ROOSEVELT TAKES OFFICE AMID THE DEPRESSION In the three years following the great stock-market crash of 1929, America's national income had plummeted more than half. While President Herbert Hoover watched, helpless, unemployment had soared to 4 million in 1930, 8 million in 1931, 12 million in 1932. More than 1 million jobless traveled the country as hobos. Clusters of jerry-built shanties known as **"Hoovervilles"** sprouted in major cities. Wall Street brokers dove headfirst from their windows, while penniless men sold apples on street corners.

Into this maelstrom of depression came a man so stricken by polio that he could only stand erect with leg braces, but he rallied the nation at his Inauguration with his decree that "the only thing we have to fear is fear itself." **Franklin D. Roosevelt,** a Democrat who promised Americans a "new deal," had won 472 electoral votes to Republican Hoover's 59. Working with a new Congress eager for bold change, F.D.R. passed 15 major legislative innovations within 100 days of taking office, and began to calm America with his masterly radio addresses, the **"fireside chats."**

1932 New President F.D.R. and wife Eleanor

Over time, many of the New Deal's more radical experiments failed or faltered—or were ruled unconstitutional by a Supreme Court Roosevelt derided as nine old men. But others, no matter how controversial at the time, were sewn into the warp and woof of American life. Social Security, a guaranteed minimum wage, insured bank deposits, the right to join a labor union—these legacies of the New Deal endure. Under F.D.R.—in a process accelerated by the massive mobilization required to win World War II—Washington shouldered the task of managing the U.S. society and economy. While later generations would back away from Big Government, there was no denying that the crippled Roosevelt had put a stricken America back on its feet. ■

UNCLE SAM'S KITCHEN
Under Roosevelt, federal programs augmented local private charities in alleviating poverty

Gandhi's March

Far from Europe, a charismatic leader, Mohandas K. Gandhi, was leading a popular revolt in the 1930s against British rule in India that would conclude in 1947 with the loss of the British Empire's greatest colony. In January 1931 TIME named Gandhi Man of the Year for 1930 and succinctly outlined his achievements: "It was exactly 12 months ago that Gandhi's Indian National Congress promulgated the

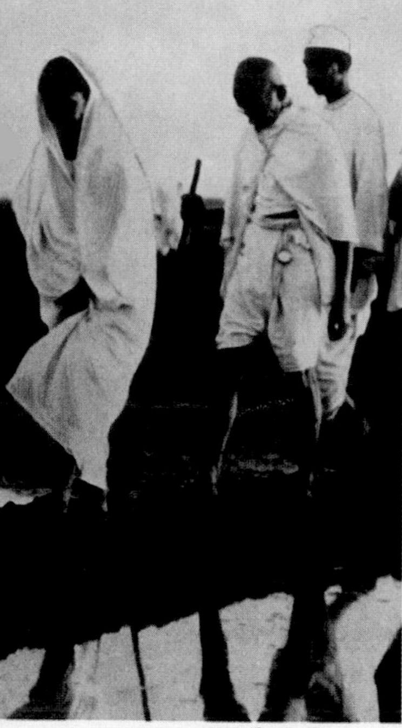

GANDHI *on the "salt march" to protest British tax policy*

Declaration of Indian Independence. It was in March that he marched to the sea to defy Britain's salt tax... It was in May that Britain jailed Gandhi. Last week he was still there, and 30,000 members of his movement were caged elsewhere. The British Empire was still wondering fearfully what to do about its most staggering problem."

REHEARSAL FOR A BLOODLETTING

JULY 18, 1936: CIVIL WAR IN SPAIN

In the 1930s many European nations were seduced by totalitarianism, and their leaders were seduced by title inflation. Germans had *der Führer,* Adolf Hitler. Italians had *il Duce,* Benito Mussolini. And fascist-leaning Spaniards had their *el Caudillo* (the chief), Francisco Franco.

A general much revered by Spanish rightists, Franco was one of a group of conservative military men who plotted a revolution against the unstable republic that had led Spain since the overthrow of King Alfonso XIII in 1931. Shortly after Franco led troops from Morocco to challenge the republic in July 1936, he became the leader of the right-wing cause.

Spain in the 1930s emerged as a cauldron in which the political movements contending for international power were thrown together, where right-wing fascists battled left-wing communists and anarchists in the street. Its war became a rehearsal for the larger battles to come: Franco's rightist forces, the Nationalists, were heavily supplied with troops, arms and airplanes by both Mussolini and Hitler, while the republic's allies—the Loyalists—were aided by antifascists of every stripe, from communist sympathizers who took their orders from Josef Stalin in Moscow to engaged intellectuals such as the writers **George Orwell, André Malraux** and **Ernest Hemingway.**

The war was savage. As TIME recounted when it was still young, "Spain's atrocity-spangled Civil War burned and butchered into its second month this week... 25,000 had been killed and less than half of these had died on any battlefield. Night after night all over Spain men were torn from their weeping families, lined up and shot for what were supposed to be their political opinions." The war ended in 1939 with Franco victorious—and with 200,000 Spaniards dead, 1 million disabled and 500,000 living in exile abroad. ■

IL DUCE **Mussolini seized power in 1922**

RIGHT FACE! In Spain, as in Germany and Italy, many people embraced fascism

HEIL HITLER!

MARCH 12, 1938: THE NAZIS OCCUPY AUSTRIA Adolf Hitler was a product of World War I and the Treaty of Versailles. When the war ended, the 29-year-old Austrian corporal lay in a hospital northeast of Berlin, partly blinded by mustard gas, raging at the nation's defeat. He threw in with an outfit called the German Labor Party and began making speeches, denouncing Bolsheviks, the Jews, the French. In 1923 he organized an absurd "Beer-Hall Putsch"; he was arrested, tried and served nine months in prison, where he wrote his racist call to arms, *Mein Kampf.* As a starving Germany suffered through the 1920s, Hitler formed the National Socialist Party, and by 1932 the Nazi demagogue was poised for power.

NOVEMBER 9, 1938 On *Kristallnacht* the Nazis smashed Jewish-owned stores, killing 91

On January 30, 1933, Hitler became Chancellor of Germany and began building his "Third Reich." All political parties were banned. Strikes were banned. Even books were banned—then burned in the streets. Jews were barred from public office and the civil service. The best and brightest of Germans—**Thomas Mann, Albert Einstein, Walter Gropius**—left the country.

Now Hitler was prepared to avenge Versailles, and in a Europe still haunted by the slaughter of World War I, there was little mood to resist his arms buildup and his advances. In 1936 he sent his mighty, modern army to occupy the supposedly demilitarized Rhineland. No one called his bluff: the Allies preferred "appeasement"—negotiation—to fighting. By 1938 Hitler had formed an alliance with a fellow dictator, Italy's **Benito Mussolini,** and launched a "war of nerves" against the flaccid Austrian government that resulted in the unification, or **Anschluss,** of Germany with Austria. His next target: Czechoslovakia. He achieved his goal when the British Prime Minister, **Neville Chamberlain,** agreed to dismember Czechoslovakia in exchange for the false promise of "peace for our time." ■

MARCH 12, 1938
Hitler is welcomed by ecstatic Austrians as he enters the city limits of Vienna in triumph

“So vast were the issues broached at Munich that no man can say with firm assurance whether history will record it as a first

HITLER & CHAMBERLAIN
Or—cat and canary?

great stride on the road to peace or as a first great slip on the road toward world war. Any man could see last week, however, that in itself the Munich agreement was not a trade. To give a man a quarter to watch your car because you believe he will slash your tires unless you do is not a trade. At Munich it was impossible to call the police, as Neville Chamberlain would have done in the Municipality of Birmingham, if Adolf Hitler had offered to slash tires. There are no international police.”

—TIME, OCTOBER 17, 1938

SEPTEMBER LIGHTNING

SEPTEMBER 1, 1939: GERMANY INVADES POLAND Treachery, lies and murder—these were the hallmarks of Adolf Hitler's launching of World War II. The night before his army commenced its surprise attack on Poland, 12 prisoners in a German concentration camp were dressed in Polish army uniforms and killed, their bodies dumped near the border. Hitler claimed these "Polish casualties" had died trying to invade Germany. With this bogus birthright the century's deadliest war was born.

At the pre-established moment of 4:45 a.m., Hitler's armies lashed out all along the 1,750-mile Polish frontier. The catastrophic war of revenge that he alone had sought was finally his to command. German troops—1.5 million men in all, led by a fearsome new military force, the 2,700 fast-moving **panzers** (tanks) of the German armored divisions, sliced deep into Polish soil. Bombers of the German ***Luftwaffe*** (air force) virtually wiped out the entire Polish air force on the ground, while dive bombers tore up railroad lines and roads; they bore devices that emitted screams to spread terror among their victims. The dawn surprise, the rampaging panzers, the shrieking dive bombers—all were elements in a bold new mode of warfare: the blitzkrieg, or lightning attack.

JUNE 1940 At the apex of his career, Hitler plays tourist in conquered Paris

Almost immediately, Britain and France declared war on Germany, whose drive to the east had been made possible by the supremely cynical **nonaggression pact** that Stalin's U.S.S.R. had agreed to only a week before the blitzkrieg. A quiet, uneasy winter followed the late-September surrender of Poland, but on May 10, Hitler moved west. His panzers rolled easily over the Netherlands, then smashed through the French army. By mid-June the ecstatic Führer was celebrating his victory in Paris, and Versailles was avenged. ■

The Nazis struck with planes, with panzers and, here in Bydgoszcz, with motorcycles

“As the bomb of the German-Russian pact exploded ... sky-high went the wreckage in a spectacle unprecedented: bits of old illusions, old securities, old trusts—pieces of Communist doctrine—crumbling fragments of Nazi propaganda—hopeful beliefs of humble people, with

STALIN & VON RIBBENTROP
Their pact sealed Poland's fate

here & there a genuine casualty—diplomatic usages, conventions, complacency, the advocates of appeasement, the believers in Hitler as a bulwark against Communism, the believers in Communism as a bulwark against Hitler, newspapermen, diplomats, intelligence officers, liberals, a skyful of hopefuls lit by the lurid glare of reality. The roar was terrific. Gleefully in Berlin Nazis gazed, spellbound and wondering, at the Führer's mighty handiwork.”

—TIME, SEPTEMBER 4, 1939

“At 3:30 Prime Minister Neville Chamberlain entered the House of Commons, looking even thinner of face than usual. At 3:47 the bulky frame of his First Lord of the Admiralty and long-time political enemy, Winston Churchill, appeared ... far into the evening Chamberlain sat and listened to critics who became more & more insistent that he resign ... the greatest

WINSTON CHURCHILL
Prime Minister at last

ovation of the day went to long-dead Oliver Cromwell, with whose angry words to the Long Parliament of 1640-53 insurgent Tory Leopold Amery closed his speech: ‘You have sat too long here for any good you have been doing. Depart, I say. Let us have done with you. In the the name of God, go!’”

–TIME, MAY 20, 1940

WE HAPPY FEW These lucky Britons escaped—but some 40,000 died or were left behind

DELIVERANCE

MAY 28, 1940: THE BRITISH ARMY ESCAPES AT DUNKIRK When Hitler finally struck to his west in May 1940, he surprised the British and French by making an end run around France's elaborate defensive fortifications, the Maginot Line, and sweeping through the "impenetrable" Ardennes Forest. After only 10 days of fighting, German panzers reached the English Channel. They raced up the coast, seized Calais and neared Dunkirk—then halted, by Adolf Hitler's personal order; for once, the Führer was cautious.

The delay allowed the British to save their army. While the Royal Navy sent 165 ships, London issued an emergency call for everything that could float—yachts, fishing boats, excursion steamers, fire-fighting boats, some 850 vessels in all—to cross the 50 miles between England and Dunkirk. The first 25,000 men reached safety by May 28, and then the odd rescue fleet hurried back for more. For nine days, often under heavy German air fire, the great evacuation continued, rescuing not only 200,000 British troops but 140,000 Allied forces as well.

Now Hitler prepared for his next conquest, the invasion of isolated England. But first he commanded the Luftwaffe to destroy the British air force—and the people's morale. In the **Battle of Britain,** the first battle fought only in the skies, outnumbered British airmen held off waves of heavy Luftwaffe bombers. Roused by a new leader, **Winston Churchill,** Londoners braved the airborne blitz with great courage, though 30,000 died before the raids ceased in the spring of 1941. For the first time, the Führer had lost a battle. ■

CLOSE CALL But London's Tower Bridge is *not* falling down

DAY OF INFAMY

DECEMBER 7, 1941: THE JAPANESE ATTACK PEARL HARBOR The brass band on the stern of the U.S.S. *Nevada* kept on playing *The Star-Spangled Banner* for the 8 a.m. flag raising, even after a Japanese bomber roared overhead and fired a torpedo at the nearby *Arizona.* The torpedo missed, but the bomber sprayed machine-gun fire at the *Nevada's* band and tore up its ensign. "This is the best goddam drill the Army Air Force has ever put on," said an *Arizona* sailor. But it was no drill: just as the Japanese had begun the Russo-Japanese War of 1904 with a surprise attack on the Russian fleet, they declared war against the U.S. with a deadly raid on the unsuspecting U.S. Pacific fleet, anchored at Pearl Harbor on the Hawaiian island of Oahu, killing 2,433 Americans and destroying 18 warships and 188 airplanes.

GUADALCANAL For G.I.s in the Pacific, the jungle was as much an enemy as the Japanese

At the same time, Japanese bombers struck Manila in the Philippines and the key cities of Singapore and Hong Kong. The Japanese, who had been fighting in mainland China since 1937, had made common cause with European dictators Hitler and Mussolini to form the **Axis powers** in 1940, and they were determined to control the Pacific. On December 8, President Roosevelt denounced the Japanese act to Congress as "a date which will live in infamy," and the U.S. declared war on Japan. In the Pacific theater, smashing U.S. naval victories at the battles of **Midway** and the **Coral Sea** took the Japanese navy out of combat, and the war assumed the form of a deadly game of hopscotch, as U.S. Marines landed on island after island, driving the Japanese back at a terrible cost to both sides. ■

SITTING DUCKS
Aircraft at Pearl Harbor's Naval Air Station were easy targets for the 183 Japanese planes above

"Beside the highway into Dachau there runs a spur line off the Munich railroad. Here a soldier stopped us and said, 'I think you better take a look at these box-cars.'

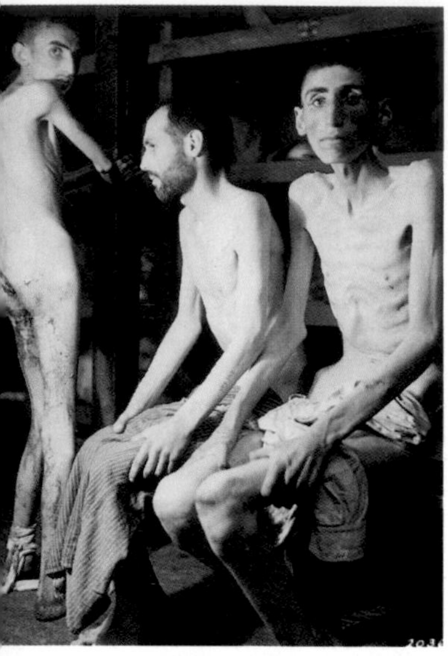

HOLOCAUST SURVIVORS
32,000 were freed at Dachau

The cars were filled with dead men. Most of them were naked. On their bony, emaciated backs and rumps were whip marks. Most of the cars were open-top cars like American coal cars. I walked among these cars and counted 39 of them which were filled with these dead. The smell was very heavy. I cannot estimate with any reasonable accuracy the number of dead we saw here, but I counted bodies in two cars and there were 53 in one and 64 in another. Now we began to meet some of the liberated ... several hundred hysterical, unshaven, lice-bitten, typhus-infected men."

—TIME, MAY 7, 1945

THE FIRST WAVE
Each G.I. carried 70 lbs. of gear into the choppy surf off Normandy

DAWN COMES UP LIKE THUNDER

JUNE 6, 1944: THE ALLIES INVADE EUROPE ON D-DAY Since the darkest days of 1941 and 1942 the Allies had regained a great deal. Hitler had launched a devastating surprise attack against his "ally," the Soviet Union, in June 1941, but in January 1943 the Soviets had held firm in the critical Battle of Stalingrad. The Anglo-American invasion of North Africa in the autumn of 1942 had also provided a needed boost to Allied morale.

Now, two years later, the Soviets had smashed all the way to the Polish frontier; the Allies had landed in Italy and pushed northward to the gates of Rome; fleets of Allied bombers were steadily pulverizing all the major cities of Germany. But Hitler's battle-hardened force of 7 million men still dominated an empire extending 1,300 miles from the Atlantic to the Dnieper. In the largest amphibious landing ever attempted, **Operation Overlord,** the Allies launched the offensive that would doom Hitler's Reich.

Led by U.S. General **Dwight D. Eisenhower,** the invasion began on the night of June 5, as planes carrying 24,000 paratroopers set off from England. At 6:30 the next morning the sea off the German-held coast of Normandy suddenly appeared full of ships—some 5,000 vessels of every variety—that landed an attack force of 154,000 men. Though they suffered 10,000 casualties, the Allies managed to secure a toehold on the beach. As reinforcements arrived, the end of Hitler's empire at last drew near. Eleven months later, Berlin would be reduced to ruins, Hitler would be a suicide, and his darkest infamy—the concentration camps—would be opened to the world. ■

MAY 2, 1945 The Soviet flag flies over the ruins of shattered Berlin as Hitler's Third Reich finally falls

ACCIDENT OF HISTORY Nagasaki was bombed because the first target, the city of Kokura, was obscured by clouds

GROUND ZERO

AUGUST 1945: U.S. ATOM BOMBS LEVEL TWO JAPANESE CITIES At the end, a trinity of bombs brought the war in Asia to a close: Jumbo, the device detonated in Alamogordo, New Mexico, to prove that atomic weapons could be made; Little Boy, the uranium titan that vaporized Hiroshima on August 6, 1945; and Fat Man, the plutonium monster that laid waste to Nagasaki three days later. In the crematory light of those blasts, the world changed—so much death contained in so little, so much of the bloody business of war refined to a bloodless decision. And only one nation—the U.S.—had the Bomb.

DEFEAT **The Japanese surrendered aboard the U.S.S. *Missouri***

President **Harry Truman** heard of Jumbo's detonation while meeting with the victorious Allied leaders in Potsdam, outside devastated Berlin. On July 30, Truman gave the order to drop Little Boy on Japan. By August 5, the device—9,700 lbs. and 10½ ft. long—was being loaded into the bomb bay of a B-29, which was christened ***Enola Gay*** after pilot Paul Tibbets' mother. At 2:45 the next morning, seven U.S. B-29s took off from Tinian, a small island in the Marianas 1,500 miles south of Japan; at 8:16 a.m. the Bomb exploded 1,900 ft. above Hiroshima.

Temperatures near the center of the explosion surged to figures ranging from 5,400°F to 7,200°F. Of the city's 76,000 buildings, only 6,000 were undamaged. An estimated 100,000 Japanese died the first day; the toll climbed in the years that followed. On August 9, Fat Man, with twice the power of Little Boy, was dropped on Nagasaki, killing some 74,000. On August 15, the Japanese surrendered. ■

“In the captain’s cabin of the 77-ft. PT-41 he lay on the tiny bunk, beaten, burning with defeat. Corregidor was doomed and with it the Philippines, but one leading actor in the most poignant tragedy in U.S. military history would be missing when the curtain fell. Douglas MacArthur, Field

MACARTHUR’S RETURN
"I shall"—and he did

Marshal of the Philippine Army, four-star General in the U.S. Army, had left the stage. It was the order of his commander in chief. But he was not really beaten. In Adelaide he made the promise that the U.S., bewildered and shaken by the Japs’ victorious campaign, heard with renewed hope: “I came through—and I shall return.” That was in in mid-March 1942. Last week, on the flag bridge of the 10,000-ton, light cruiser *Nashville,* stood a proud, erect figure in freshly pressed khaki. Douglas MacArthur had come back to the Philippines, as he had promised.”

—TIME, OCTOBER 30, 1944

Reveilles in Asia

1947 *Muslims with a dead Hindu in newly free India*

Two long-fought battles for freedom in Asia were resolved in the wake of World War II. On August 15, 1947, India was cut loose from its 132-year-old status as a British colony to become an independent nation. But freedom was marred by religious violence, and many Indian Muslims immigrated to Pakistan, a new Islamic nation carved out of India's northwest. In China, Mao Zedong's long march to unify his nation under communism succeeded when he took Beijing in January 1949. With vast China joining Stalin's Soviet Union in the Marxist camp, cold war fears of "the reds" escalated in America.

1949 *Mao's victorious Red Army marches into Beijing*

CHILD OF WAR
Rachel Levy, 7, runs from Arab fire in the Old City in Jerusalem

BIRTH PAINS

MAY 14, 1948: ISRAEL BECOMES A NATION From the ashes of Hitler's Holocaust, in the harsh sands of Middle Eastern deserts, on land sacred to its scattered people for two millenniums of wandering, the tiny nation of Israel was born in 1948, elbowing itself into being in a hostile part of the world by combining its own energy and the world's sympathy. Israel willed its existence defiantly—by force of arms and by proclaiming independence for itself, by defeating five encircling armies and forcing the signatures of neighboring Arab nations to a U.N.-sponsored armistice.

Shortly after sunrise on May 14, the Union Jack flapped down from its staff over Government House, on Jerusalem's Hill of Evil Counsel, ending the British mandate over Palestine after 26 years. At 4 p.m. **David Ben-Gurion,** the longtime leader of the Jewish settlers, or Zionists, who had flocked to Palestine from Europe, proclaimed "the establishment of the Jewish State in Palestine, to be called Israel." In the two hours left before sundown, when the Jewish Sabbath would begin, the jubilant citizens of Tel Aviv danced in the streets, paraded with blue-and-white Star of David flags, prayed in their synagogues.

The United States immediately recognized Israel. Its Muslim neighbors, however, united as the **Arab League,** welcomed the new nation with an attack, as troops moved in from Transjordan and Lebanon, Egypt and Syria. But the tough Jewish underground army, the Haganah, hardened from years of fighting to protect Jewish settlements in Palestine, stymied the Arabs. By the summer of 1949 all its enemies had signed cease-fires brokered by the U.N., and Israel was secure—for the moment. ■

FIRE! Arab shells pound a Jewish-held house in Jerusalem

NATIONS

WINGED VICTORY

JUNE 26, 1948: THE BERLIN AIRLIFT

The incessant roar of the planes—that typical and terrible 20th century sound, a voice of cold, mechanized anger—filled every street in Berlin. It reverberated in the hollow houses; it throbbed in the weary minds of the people, who were bitter, afraid, but far from broken; it echoed in intently listening ears in the Kremlin. The sound meant the West was standing its ground and fighting back in a new kind of war, the **cold war.**

RED SCARE Senator Joseph McCarthy, right, exploited cold war fears to turn the U.S. into a paranoid state

The West had teamed with its ideological foe, Stalin's U.S.S.R., to defeat the common enemy, Adolf Hitler. But Germany's utter destruction in the conflict created a power vacuum in Central Europe, and Stalin rushed to impose Soviet hegemony "from Stettin in the Baltic to Trieste in the Adriatic," in the words of Britain's Winston Churchill, who memorably christened the Soviet power zone an **Iron Curtain.**

The cold war would define geopolitics until the Soviet Empire dissolved in the early 1990s. Berlin, occupied after the war by the four Allied powers (the U.S., Britain, France and the U.S.S.R.) but lying within the Soviet region, became a flash point where the Soviets tested Western resolve, again and again.

In 1948 the battle for allegiance was fought in the hearts and minds of Berliners—but most of all in their bellies. When the three Western Allies united their occupation sectors to create a new West Germany, the Soviets blockaded access to the city, attempting to starve into submission the 2.5 million people in the city's Western zones. The Allies vowed to feed them, by air. In **Operation Vittles** (the G.I.s' term) they landed a plane every six minutes, 24 hours a day—until the Soviets lifted the blockade after 318 days. ■

SPECIAL DELIVRY

The final tally: 200,000 individual air flights; 1.5 million tons of food and supplies received

BITTER BATTLES IN A COLD WAR

JUNE 25, 1950: WAR BEGINS IN KOREA

The cold war was a global struggle that could—and did—erupt on a score of fronts, from Berlin to the Bay of Pigs, from the Congo to the Korean peninsula. It was in Korea, divided into a communist North and a pro-Western South at the close of World War II, that the two ideological adversaries, initially acting through proxies, first met in actual combat.

In June the Soviet-equipped North Korean People's army crossed the border at the 38th parallel and invaded the Republic of South Korea, quickly taking the capital, Seoul. With the Soviets boycotting, the new U.N. Security Council voted to undertake its first "police action" and sent a U.S.-led force commanded by World War II legend **Douglas MacArthur,** 70, to support the South. In September MacArthur led a masterly invasion at Inchon, Seoul's port, that routed the North. Said TIME: "The Inchon landing was in the great American tradition first developed in World War II. It swept around the sea anchor of the enemy flank and struck at his most vulnerable spot." By October the U.N. forces had taken Pyongyang, the North's capital, and were rolling toward the Chinese border.

But the U.S. and the U.N. badly underestimated communist **Mao Zedong,** who had united China only the year before. Mao sent hordes of fresh troops into the fray in November, delivering what TIME called "a crushing counter-offensive" that pushed the U.N. troops back all along the front in bitter winter fighting before the U.N. dug in to hold South Korea. The ugly "police action" dragged on for two more long years before it finally ended in 1953. The result: 54,000 Americans, 900,000 Chinese and 1.8 million Koreans were dead—and very little Korean land had changed hands. ■

SEPTEMBER 15, 1950 MacArthur's landing at Inchon cut off and strangled the North's army

U.S. Marines fall back before the massive Chinese advance in 1950

NATIONS

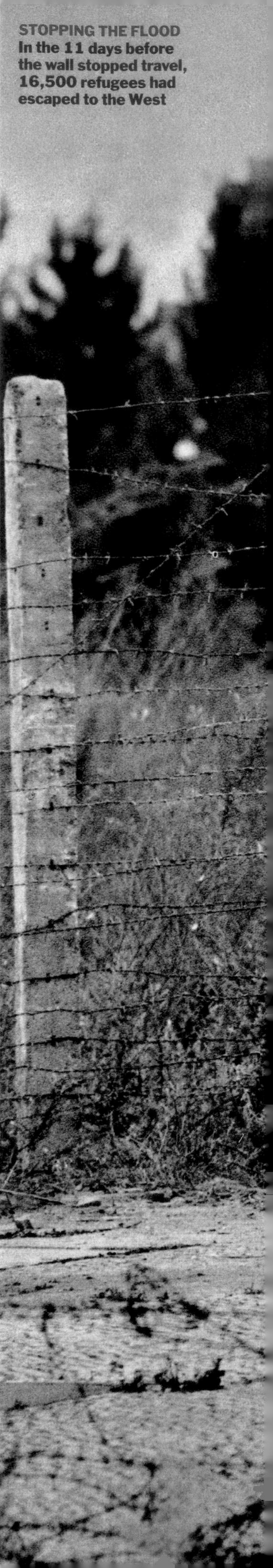

STOPPING THE FLOOD **In the 11 days before the wall stopped travel, 16,500 refugees had escaped to the West**

BORDER WARS

AUGUST 13, 1961: THE BERLIN WALL IS BUILT The clank of steel on cobblestones echoed down the mean, dark streets. Frightened East Berliners peeked from behind their curtains to see military convoys stretching for blocks: jeeps, trucks and buses crammed with grim, steel-helmeted East German soldiers. Rattling in their wake were the tanks—squat Russian-built T-34s and T-54s. At each major intersection, a platoon peeled off and ground to a halt. The rest headed on for the sector border, the 25-mile frontier that cut through the heart of Berlin like a jagged piece of glass. Cargo trucks were already unloading stone blocks, rolls of barbed wire, picks and shovels. When dawn came four hours later, a wall divided East Berlin from West. That wall was a strangely revealing emblem of the cold war, for it advertised to all the world not only the failure of East Germany's communist system, but also the subjection of a people who could only be kept within its borders by bullets, bayonets and barricades.

1956 The Soviet Union brutally quashed an uprising in Hungary

In 1961 the cold war was reaching a peak. After **Fidel Castro's** rebels won control of Cuba in January 1959, Castro had turned to the Soviets for aid, and the U.S. attempt to overthrow his regime—the invasion at the **Bay of Pigs** in April 1961—was a pitiful failure. The Berlin ploy was Soviet boss **Nikita Khrushchev's** way of testing the mettle of the young U.S. President, **John F. Kennedy.** But Kennedy backed Khrushchev down in October 1962, when he made the Soviets move missiles that threatened the U.S. out of Cuba. ■

“The executioner’s rifle cracked across Cuba last week, and around the world voices hopefully cheering for a new democracy fell still. The men who had just won a popular revolution for old ideals—for democracy, justice and honest government—themselves picked up the arrogant tools of

FIDEL CASTRO
A rebel behind a desk

dictatorship. As the public urged them on, the Cuban rebels shot more than 200 men, summarily convicted in drumhead courts, as mass murderers for the fallen Batista dictatorship. The only man who could have silenced the firing squads was Fidel Castro Ruz, 32, the lawyer, fighter and visionary who led the rebellion. And Castro was in no mood for mercy ... [He] is egotistic, impulsive, immature, disorganized. He hates desks—behind which he may have to sit to run Cuba.”

–TIME, JANUARY 26, 1959

"Inside Air Force One, the craft trembling with the vibration of its idling engines, Jackie Kennedy joined a sad and shaken group waiting for Lyndon Johnson to take his oath of office. The plane's sweltering, gold-carpeted 'living room' was crowded with 27 people. At Johnson's right was his wife Lady Bird. Behind them ranged White House staffers; the shirt cuffs of Rear Admiral George Burkley, President Kennedy's physician, bore bloodstains.

THE TRANSFER OF POWER
2:38 p.m. at Dallas' Love Field

Federal District Judge Sarah T. Hughes, a trim, tiny woman of 67 whom Kennedy had appointed to the bench in 1961, pronounced the oath in a voice barely audible over the engines. Johnson, his left hand on a small black Bible, repeated it firmly. The President leaned forward, kissed Lady Bird on the forehead."

–TIME, NOVEMBER 29, 1963

DEATH OF A PRESIDENT

NOVEMBER 22, 1963: JOHN F. KENNEDY IS ASSASSINATED His bright trajectory through life—the shining passage from boyhood wealth to PT-boat hero to the presidency at age 43—ended in midpassage, severed in a glaring Friday noontime in Dallas. John F. Kennedy's assassination remains a black hole at the center of the American century, absorbing hopes while it spins out cynicism and seemingly endless conspiracy theories.

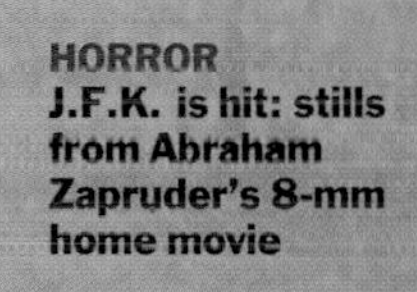

HORROR
J.F.K. is hit: stills from Abraham Zapruder's 8-mm home movie

Kennedy, in the third year of his presidency, had come to conservative Texas to shore up support for his planned run for reelection the next year. In this supposedly hostile political land he had been strongly welcomed in San Antonio, Fort Worth and Houston. At the Dallas airport, 5,000 people waved and cheered as J.F.K. and his popular wife Jacqueline entered the open limousine that would take them downtown. But at 12:30 p.m., as the car traversed Dealey Plaza, the President was struck. His body slumped to the left and blood gushed from his head. He was pronounced dead within the hour at Parkland Memorial Hospital.

By 2 p.m. Dallas police had arrested **Lee Harvey Oswald,** a political malcontent who had spent time in the Soviet Union, as the suspected assassin. But incredibly, as a stunned nation watched on TV, Oswald himself was shot on Sunday morning at Dallas police headquarters. President Lyndon Johnson named Chief Justice **Earl Warren** to lead a commission to explore Kennedy's murder; though it declared Oswald the lone assassin, millions of Americans still believe that the full story of that sad day remains to be told. ■

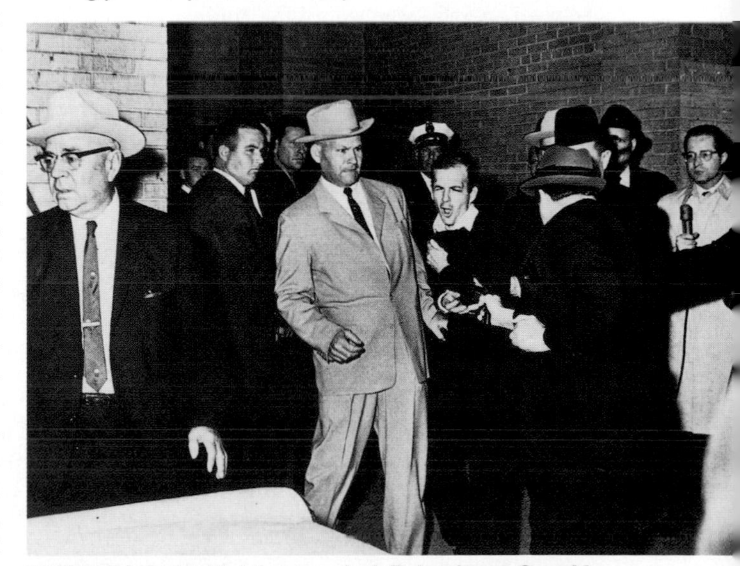

NOVEMBER 24 Nightclub owner Jack Ruby shoots Oswald

NO WAY OUT

JANUARY 30, 1968: THE TET OFFENSIVE ROCKS SOUTH VIETNAM In the small Asian nation of Vietnam the U.S. suffered its greatest defeat of the cold war. In 1954 a group of freedom fighters led by communist Ho Chi Minh defeated the French at Dien Bien Phu, ending colonialism in Vietnam. Under the terms of the 1954 Geneva peace accord, Vietnam was divided in two, pending a 1956 election. Fearing a victory for the communists, the U.S. backed South Vietnamese leader Ngo Dinh Diem's plan to stop the election. The nation remained divided, and insurgents who took their orders from Ho Chi Minh—the Viet Cong—began a guerrilla war against the South.

John F. Kennedy sent 15,500 U.S. military "advisers" into South Vietnam and helped stage the assassination of the corrupt Diem, further destabilizing the nation. **Lyndon Johnson** poured U.S. troops into the South: 22,000 in 1964 grew to more than 500,000 in 1968. The massive escalation, including heavy bombing, seemed to have no effect on North Vietnam—but it led to unrest in a troubled America, where draft-age students rebelled against the war.

Then, during the 1968 Tet, Vietnam's New Year's holiday, communists attacked 40 cities up and down the country in a smashing surprise attack. They overran Pleiku in the highlands and Ben Tre in the Mekong Delta; in Saigon, the capital, gun battles erupted in the streets. Two months later, President Johnson announced he would not run for re-election. **Richard Nixon,** who won office by vowing to end the war, escalated it with his 1970 attack on communist strongholds in Cambodia. But he managed to get the last U.S. troops out of the country by 1973, under the fig leaf of a "peace accord" with the North few believed would last. ■

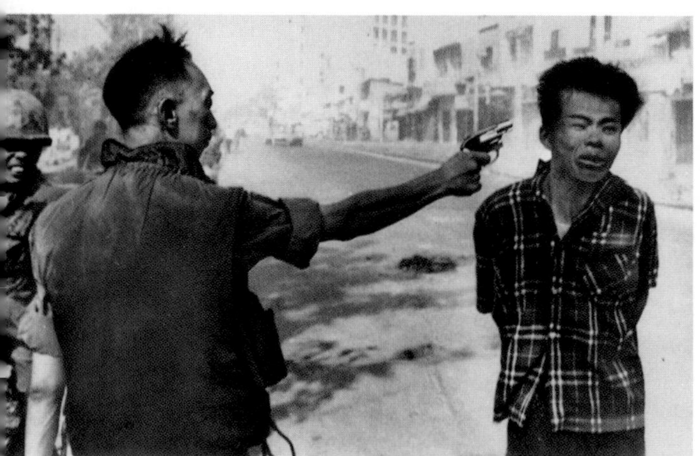

1968 A South Vietnamese police chief shoots a guerrilla

SEMPER FI Wounded U.S. Marines ride a tank doubling as an ambulance during the 1968 Tet offensive

"Once again the crackle of gunfire. Once again the long journey home, the hushed procession, the lowered flags and harrowed faces of a nation in grief. Once again the simple question: Why? The second Kennedy assassination—almost two months to the day after the murder of

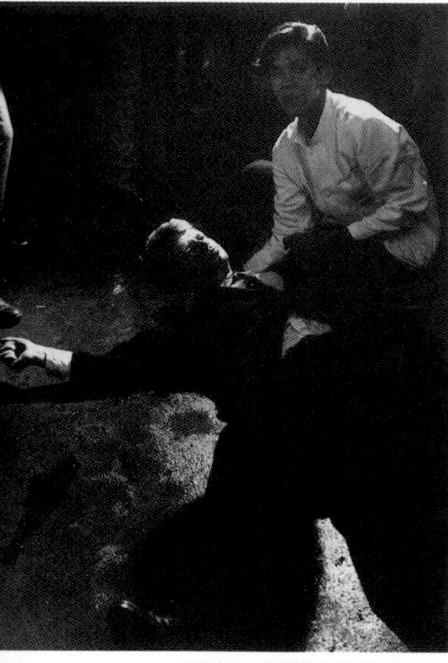

AFTER THE SHOOTING
A hotel busboy with Kennedy

Martin Luther King Jr.—immediately prompted, at home and abroad, deep doubts about the stability of America. For the young people, in particular, who had been persuaded by the new politics of Robert Kennedy and Eugene McCarthy to recommit themselves to the American electoral system, the assassination seemed to confirm all their lingering suspicions that society could not be reformed by democratic means."

–TIME, JUNE 14, 1968

SOUND RETREAT!
The airlift ran from 11 a.m. on April 29th to almost 8 a.m. the next day

LAST FLIGHT FROM SAIGON

APRIL 30, 1975: SOUTH VIETNAM FALLS

The signs of impending doom had been multiplying for at least a month. A headlong bug-out from the Central Highlands in March had signaled that South Vietnam could no longer muster either the strength or the will to hold off the armies sweeping down from the communist North. In late March, Danang, a key Southern city, fell; on April 20 the NVA (North Vietnam army) took Xuan Loc, a small town 38 miles northeast of Saigon. The next night, South Vietnam's President, **Nguyen Van Thieu,** resigned. By April 26 Saigon was surrounded—and the next day it was bombed by captured American jets.

On April 29, the U.S. Armed Forces Radio station played *White Christmas,* the signal to begin a helicopter lift of U.S. troops and citizens, as well as pro-U.S. Vietnamese, from Saigon to U.S. warships 20 miles out to sea. The lift ran for about 21 hours; the helicopter pilots flew for 10 to 15 hours straight, with each trip taking about 40 minutes in the air and some 10 to 15 minutes on the ground loading up. Said a U.S. Marine witness: "People were climbing fences. It was bedlam."

At 9 a.m. on the 30th, one hour after the last U.S. chopper lifted off, NVA columns moved into Saigon. The war had claimed the lives of 57,605 U.S. and 664,357 Vietnamese soldiers. It had divided Americans into two bitter factions, **hawks** and **doves.** It had engendered the tragic year of 1968, which saw riots in the streets at the Democratic Convention in Chicago and the murder of **Senator Robert Kennedy** as he campaigned for the presidency. At last, with a whimper, the war was over. ■

AUGUST 1968 Chicago police pound antiwar protesters

IN DEFEAT, DEFIANCE

AUGUST 9, 1974: RICHARD NIXON RESIGNS In his first words to the American people after being sworn in to succeed Richard Nixon, new President Gerald Ford said, "Our long national nightmare is over." Indeed, when President Nixon gave up his office over the various illegal activities known as Watergate, it was the first resignation of a President in history. It was also the culmination of a constitutional crisis that entangled all three branches of the government in a seemingly interminable parade of infamy: high officials marched into hearing rooms to recite tales of burglaries, "dirty tricks" and crooked campaign contributions, of powers abused, tapes erased, expletives deleted. As White House counsel **John Dean** warned Nixon before testifying against him, "There is a cancer growing on the presidency."

"A CANCER" John Dean outlines the cover-up

Republican Nixon, so adept at exploiting voters' fears of communism, harbored his own inner demons: he maintained an "enemies list," and his White House was saturated with pettiness and hatred. During his bid for re-election in 1972, his campaign staff approved the burglary of Democratic National Headquarters at Washington's Watergate complex by a team of criminal "plumbers." When the group was arrested, Nixon approved payoffs to the principals and a cover-up of his involvement that only heightened his culpability.

Slowly, the truth emerged. Reporters **Bob Woodward** and **Carl Bernstein** dug up key evidence, which was diligently pursued by Federal Judge **John Sirica** and a Senate committee chaired by **Sam Ervin.** Twelve days after the Supreme Court ruled unanimously that the President must surrender tape recordings that would prove his guilt, and five days after the House Judiciary Committee voted the articles of impeachment, Richard Nixon, a gifted yet tragic figure, resigned his office. ■

HIS LAST BOW Undaunted even in his hour of disgrace, Nixon flashes a victory sign on leaving the White House

"The jowls jiggled. The eyebrows rolled up and down. The forehead seemed seized by spasms. Yet the lips continuously courted a smile, suggesting an inner bemusement. The words tumbled out, softened by the gentle Southern tones and the folksy idiom. But he conveyed a sense of moral outrage. 'Divine right went out with the American Revolution and doesn't belong to White House aides,' the speaker said. 'That is not Executive privilege. It is Executive poppy-cock.' With those words, North Carolina's

SENATOR SAM ERVIN
Leader of the Senate inquiry

Democratic Senator Sam J. Ervin Jr. was stepping up the tempo in a showdown over secrecy between the U.S. Senate and the President. If Richard Nixon will not allow his aides to testify under oath before his committee, Ervin vowed, he will seek to have them arrested."

–TIME, APRIL 16, 1973

DESERT PROPHET

Milestones of the 1970s

TERROR IN MUNICH Pro-Palestinian terrorists shocked the world by killing 11 Israelis at the 1972 Olympic Games in Germany.

POL POT'S REIGN OF DEATH Devastated by U.S. bombing in the Vietnam War, Cambodia fell to the communist dictator Pol Pot in 1975. The radical leftist waged a campaign of genocide against his own people that claimed some 2 million lives by 1979.

THE OPEC OIL CRISIS The chiefly Arab nations of the Organization of Petroleum Exporting Countries hiked prices drastically in 1973, strangling a world grown reliant on cheap oil and gas.

CAMP DAVID SUMMIT In 1978 President Jimmy Carter sequestered Egypt's Anwar Sadat and Israel's Menachem Begin at Camp David in Maryland until they hammered out an epochal peace deal.

FEBRUARY 1, 1979: MILITANT MUSLIMS TAKE OVER IRAN It was an age-old recipe for revolution: a corrupt regime led by a greedy ruler who turned his back on his own culture; an austere, committed rebel whose power and mystique grew once he was exiled from his land. The nation was Iran in the 1970s; the ruler was **Shah Mohammed Reza Pahlavi,** a U.S. client; the rebel **Ayatullah Khomeini,** a militant Muslim holy man exiled by the Shah.

As the fundamentalist Ayatullah's clandestine tapes urging revolt spread through Iran, the Shah's peacock throne tottered. Finally, the Shah left the country in January 1979, and the Ayatullah returned from exile in France to a hero's welcome. Soon, with the aid of fundamentalist Islamic religious leaders, the **mullahs,** he would run an even stricter dictatorship than the Shah's. When fanatic anti-American students attacked the U.S. embassy in November 1979, Khomeini supported their taking of 52 hostages. It was the first act of a long-running crisis; for 444 days, Americans watched in agony as their countrymen were humiliated by their student captors. **President Jimmy Carter,** hamstrung by the situation, finally attempted a daring rescue operation that fizzled in the desert, further frustrating America. Khomeini, triumphant, held the hostages until the day Carter left office in 1981. ■

THE AYATULLAH
Khomeini's title, Ayatullah, is an honorific accorded great mullahs. Here he receives pilgrims after his dramatic 1979 return to Iran

“In the shadow of the walls of Peking's Forbidden City, the history of modern China is being written these days in foot-high ideographs of pure vitriol... The world wiped its eyes in astonishment as Mao's Great Proletarian Cultural Revolution,

RED GUARD RAMPAGE
110 million minions of Mao

aimed at “purifying” Chinese Communism, erupted into strife and stridency so bitter that it produced widespread chaos and verged on civil war. Chinese fought Chinese in the cities, and the ubiquitous ***tatzebao,*** or posters, attacked with such catholic ferocity—condemning both Mao's enemies and his lieutenants—that there may soon be no one left undenounced in all of Red China.”

–TIME, JANUARY 13, 1967

A DREAM DEFERRED Defiant protesters erected a poignant Chinese version of the Statue of Liberty

YEARNING TO BREATHE FREE

JUNE 3, 1989: MASSACRE IN TIANANMEN SQUARE It was only a matter of time. For seven weeks both Beijing's rulers and the thousands of demonstrators for democracy who had occupied the capital city's Tiananmen Square showed great restraint. And then the dream ended in a spasm of fury and blood.

China had endured much since the triumph of Mao Zedong's Red Army in 1949 ended the nation's long civil war. In the late 1950s Mao's mistitled **Great Leap Forward** produced a famine that killed millions. In 1966 he unleashed more turmoil with the **Cultural Revolution.** China reached out to the West when President Richard Nixon visited Beijing in 1972, but Mao's death in 1976 sparked a power struggle that ended only with the arrest of the **Gang of Four.**

Eventually China found stability under Mao's heir, **Deng Xiaoping,** who relaxed Mao's Marxist economic strictures while maintaining the communist regime's tight grip on human rights. But his reforms fed the hunger for personal freedom, and in April 1989 pro-democracy students began protesting in Tiananmen Square. Growing bolder, they announced a hunger strike on May 13; the government declared martial law on May 20. A watching world held its breath as brave Chinese defied Deng's tanks with their bodies.

Finally Deng moved. A convoy of 50 trucks loaded with foot soldiers barreled through Beijing's crowded streets at 2 a.m. on Sunday, June 3. Suddenly soldiers of the People's Liberation Army, ten thousand strong, mounted a deliberately vicious assault. Leveling their AK-47 assault rifles, soldiers began firing away at the mobs. Huge streams of people fled in terror. Some protesters held fast, fighting with rocks and Molotov cocktails until the end. The death toll, still unknown, was probably in the thousands. Deng the reformer had sought refuge in a hoary Maoist maxim: "Political power grows out of the barrel of a gun." ■

FEBRUARY 1972 Richard Nixon visits Beijing

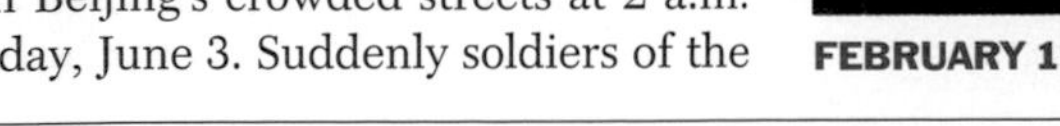

COLD WAR HOT SPOTS

JULY 17, 1979: SANDINISTA REBELS TAKE POWER IN NICARAGUA When corrupt dictator Anastasio Somoza Debayle, a U.S. client, was driven from Nicaragua after a long civil war, the rebel Sandinistas took over the government—and the war intensified, as Somoza supporters and other Sandinista foes formed a right-wing guerrilla army, the ***contras.*** When the Sandinista regime turned to Moscow for aid, U.S. President **Ronald Reagan** began arming and funding the *contras.* Though Reagan called the *contras* "freedom fighters," their terror tactics and documented human-rights abuses led Congress to cut off aid to their cause. The White House turned to covert action, and in 1986 its **"Iran-*contra*"** scheme was revealed: under Lieut. Colonel Oliver North, a National Security Council aide, money from illegal sales of U.S. missiles to terrorist state Iran had in turn been illegally channeled to the *contras.* In 1990 moderate **Violeta Barrios de Chamorro** was elected President of Nicaragua in a vote for normality. ■

Milestones of the 1980s

AFGHANISTAN
The Soviet Union sent troops into an Afghan civil war late in 1979, but many Soviet soldiers died at the hands of U.S.-backed guerrillas, the Muslim *mujahedin*—at left, with a captured chopper. The Soviets did not withdraw from the quagmire until 1989.

POLAND
Lech Walesa, a young electrician from the shipyards of Gdansk, led a successful labor strike in 1980 that signaled the beginnin of the end of Soviet dominance in Poland. Walesa went on to lea Solidarity, the labor union that united Pol against the U.S.S.R.

THE FALKLANDS
In April 1982, troops from Argentina took over the tiny Falkland Islands—home to 1,800 Britons. Defiant Prime Minister Margaret Thatcher sent an armada of 100 ships to the islands; after a brief war, the Union Jack was back in place by mid-June.

WASHINGTON
In 1986 Oliver North, mastermind of the White House's covert Iran-*contra* operation, testified before a Senate committee. A hero to some, a scoundrel to others, North was convicted of a felony, but the decision was later reversed on appeal.

"*Mikhail Gorbachev.* The name, the beaming, birthmarked visage and the outstretched, crowd-caressing hand have become so familiar in the past 33 months that it is difficult to remember the man's predecessors. Vague images come to mind of stone-faced figures frozen in mid-frown atop the Lenin Mausoleum. Gargoyles in fur hats. Perhaps Gorbachev's most obvious accomplishment is that he has reinvented the idea of the Soviet leader. Virtually everything about his country and its place in world affairs seems less ponderous, less opaque than it did before he became General

MIKHAIL GORBACHEV
Man of the Year 1987

Secretary of the Communist Party... Perhaps the reverie will end... Even so, Gorbachev's reforms can no longer be dismissed as a mere matter of style."

–TIME, JANUARY 4, 1988

AND THE WALL CAME . . .

NOVEMBER 9, 1989: THE FALL OF THE BERLIN WALL For 28 years it had stood as the symbol of the division of Europe and the world, of communist suppression, of the xenophobia of a regime that had to lock its people in lest they be tempted by another, freer life—the Berlin Wall, that hideous, 28-mile-long scar through the heart of a once proud European capital, not to mention the soul of a people. And then—*poof!*—it was gone. It was one of those rare times when the tectonic plates of history shift beneath men's feet, and nothing after is quite the same.

In October 1989 fed-up East Germans began streaming into the West through Hungary by the thousands, and when the nation's new government relaxed travel restrictions, citizens grew bolder. At the stroke of midnight on November 9, the thousands gathered on both sides of the Wall let out a great roar and started going through it, as well as up and over it; the Wall seemed to disappear in a great sea of humanity. They tooted on trumpets; they danced; they hauled out hammers and whacked away at it—and the Wall came tumbling down. In rapid order, so did the East German government's Cabinet and the Communist Party Politburo.

Thus East Germany joined other states behind the Iron Curtain that had shrugged off the Soviet yoke in the late 1980s in a series of revolutions that was almost eerily peaceful. Ironically, the movement began in Moscow; when new Soviet leader **Mikhail Gorbachev** came to power in 1985, he launched his radical policies of ***glasnost*** (openness) and ***perestroika*** (restructuring). But his reforms only sparked the desire for more freedom, and across the Soviet bloc, communist governments began to wither away: in **Hungary** in 1988, in both **Poland** and **Czechoslovakia** in 1989. In the end, the Soviet Union itself dissolved on the 31st of December, 1991, after an August coup by hardliners was foiled by a more radical democrat than Gorbachev—**Boris Yeltsin.** ■

VACLAV HAVEL The dissident Czech playwright led a "velvet revolution"

TAKE THAT! Amid toasts and taunts, Germans destroyed the 28-mile-long barrier

BOMBS OVER BAGHDAD

JANUARY 17, 1991: WAR BEGINS IN THE PERSIAN GULF The war known as Desert Storm, which pitted an international alliance of allies against the aggressive Iraq of strongman Saddam Hussein, was necessary. But it was also a bit unreal, an action-adventure that, like most movies, was divided into three chapters, with decisive turning points: first the August 1990 invasion of Kuwait by Saddam; then the onset of the air war, with the night bombing of Baghdad by the allies in January; and finally the ground war and the end game. But the victory was unsatisfying; Saddam was driven from Kuwait, but the dictator remained in power in Baghdad when the allies withdrew.

Saddam, a virulent enemy of the West who had ruled Iraq with an iron fist since 1971, sent his forces south into neighboring Kuwait on August 2, 1990, and took over the nation's prized oil fields. U.S. President **George Bush** quickly formed an international coalition that issued a January 15 deadline for Iraq to withdraw. Syria, Saudi Arabia, Japan and many other nations were part of the allied group.

The deadline passed, and just two days later the allies began the war with a high-tech air raid on Saddam's capital. A spellbound world tuned in to the Cable News Network to see—live—U.S. Stealth bombers and Tomahawk cruise missiles slamming into Baghdad. It was clear that Saddam was overmatched. But he now played his worst card, launching Soviet-built **Scud missiles** at Israel, the West's chief ally in the Mideast, and killing four Israelis. Later, 28 Americans would die when a Scud hit an air-base in Saudi Arabia.

SADDAM Beaten—but still standing

That was the extent of Saddam's success. On February 23, the allies, led by American General **Norman Schwarzkopf,** sent some 150,000 allied troops streaming into Iraq-held Kuwait. Iraqi soldiers surrendered en masse, and within 100 hours the war was over. A beaten Saddam, in a last act of revenge, had his soldiers put Kuwait's oil fields to the torch as they withdrew. ■

ASSAULT ON SADDAM **More than 2,000 warplanes from six allied nations hit Iraq on the first night of the war**

MIDDLEMAN
U.S. influence was essential in brokering the peace agreement

HISTORY IN A HANDSHAKE

SEPTEMBER 13, 1993: ISRAEL MAKES PEACE WITH THE PALESTINIANS History is often the residue of tanks and armies. Sometimes it is the work of paper and pens. But when veteran antagonists Yasser Arafat and Yitzhak Rabin clasped hands in front of a beaming Bill Clinton on the White House lawn in 1993, history was forged in a hand shake. The seemingly unbelievable scene was beamed to millions of people in a world nurtured for 45 years on a diet of hatred and death in the arid lands of the Israelis and Arabs. There stood Arafat, the chairman of the Palestine Liberation Organization, whose drive for a homeland for his people had led him to make common cause with terrorists, shaking hands with Israel's Prime Minister, Rabin, the former army chief of staff whose victory in the Six-Day War had greatly expanded Israel's land. The parchment they signed was a framework for interim Palestinian self-government, as well as a document that bound Israel and the Palestine Liberation Organization to further deliberation.

The handshake was the culmination of months of secret negotiations first undertaken by free-lance Palestinian and Israeli peacemakers, not diplomats. It was the biggest thaw in the Middle East since an earlier visionary, Egypt's **Anwar Sadat,** had made peace with Israel's **Menachem Begin** in 1978. But Sadat had paid a price for being the first leader of an Arab nation to recognize Israel since the birth of the Jewish state: he was assassinated in 1981. Sadly, Rabin shared Sadat's fate; he was killed in 1995 by a right-wing Jewish zealot as he addressed a Jerusalem peace rally. ■

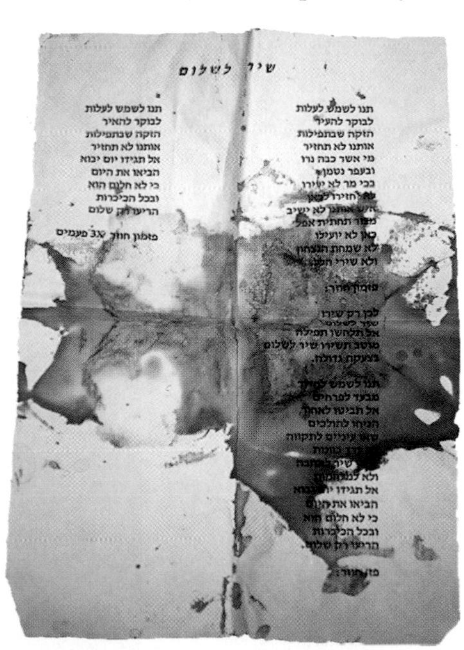

שיר לשלום

תנו לשמש לעלות
לבוקר להאיר
הזכה שבתפילות
אותנו לא תחזיר
אל תגידו יום יבוא
הביאו את היום
כי לא חלום הוא
ובכל הכיכרות

תנו לשמש לעלות
לבוקר להעיר
הזכה שבתפילות
אותנו לא תחזיר
מי אשר כבה נרו
ובעפר נטמן

SONG OF PEACE **Rabin's lyric sheet for the Israeli anthem was bloodied by his murder**

FREE AT LAST

APRIL 1994: APARTHEID ENDS IN SOUTH AFRICA It was a spectacle of true transformation: during one memorable week in April, in a series of astonishing episodes beginning with all-race voting, the old South Africa of apartheid and oppression peacefully dissolved itself and re-emerged as a hopeful, newly democratic nation. The old order formally ended as cheering crowds of both blacks and whites in the nine new provincial capitals hailed the lowering of apartheid's blue-white-and-orange flag and the raising of a banner with six colors symbolizing the people, their blood, their land, the gold under the ground, the sky—and peace.

On that day the white minority government, still with a monopoly grip on political power, handed over control of the country to the black majority it had held in servitude for 300 years. The white rulers had methodically segregated blacks, paid them a pittance, ignored their housing and barely pretended to educate them. In 1948 whites had adopted apartheid, their most racist policy, which strictly stratified their society by color.

Two visionary leaders share the credit for South Africa's historic evolution. The first was a lawyer/activist of black royal blood, **Nelson Mandela,** who was jailed for 27 years for his violent opposition to apartheid. Over his long incarceration, Mandela became a mythic figure: an inspiration to blacks and a recrimination to whites. When finally freed from prison in 1990, he moved the world by his dignity and his willingness to forgive his captors in order to unite his nation.

MANDELA In captivity for 27 years

The second figure in South Africa's transformation was the white President who freed Mandela, **F.W. de Klerk.** In the face of strong opposition from many entrenched whites, De Klerk negotiated with Mandela for two years to end apartheid, enfranchise blacks and make the election possible. When the ballots were counted, there was no surprise but much rejoicing: by a huge margin, Nelson Mandela was chosen the new President of his reborn land. ■

PARTY LINE
After waiting years to vote, blacks in Soweto celebrated with long lines at the polls

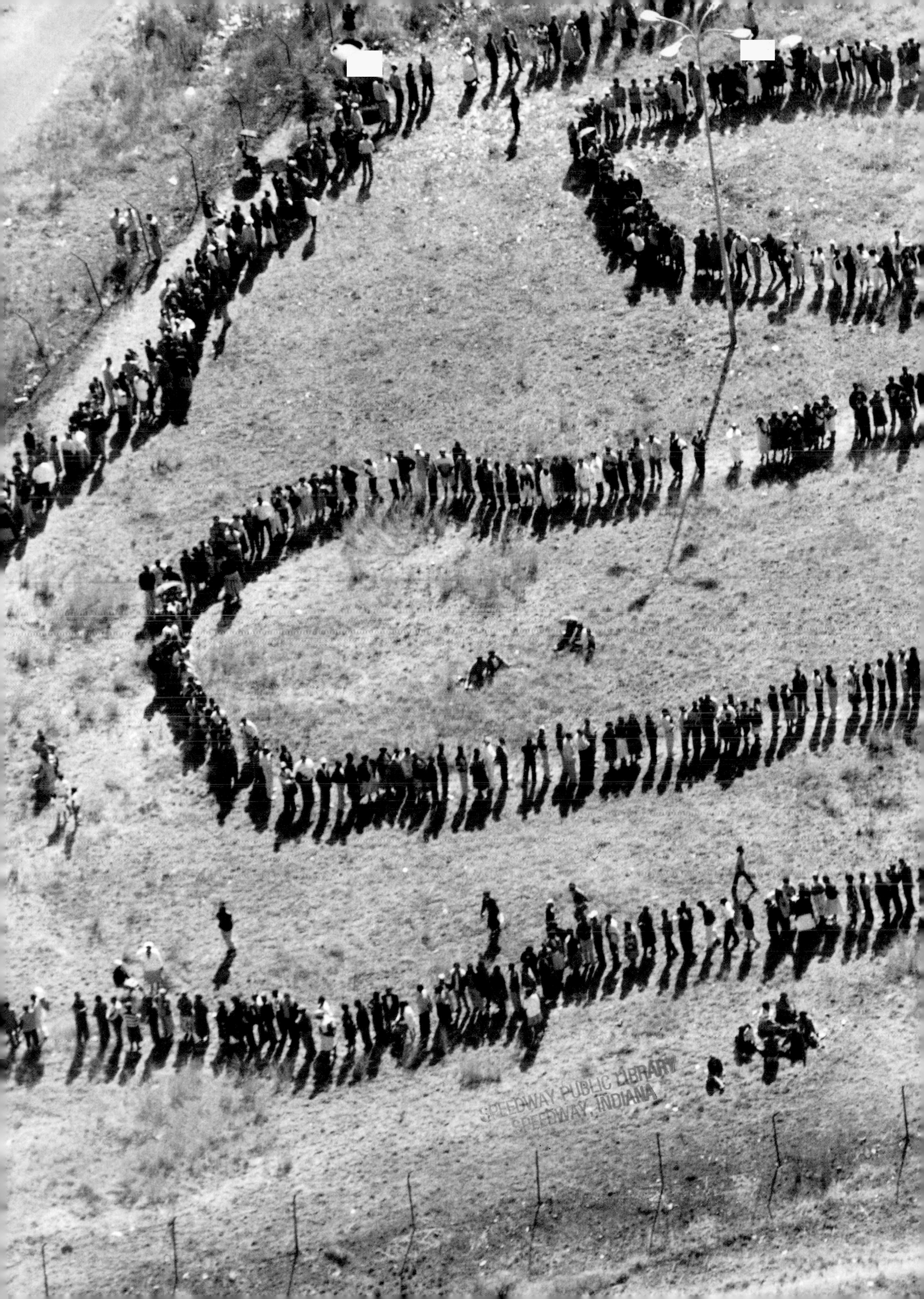

CONVICTED But McVeigh showed no remorse

A BLOW TO THE HEART

APRIL 19, 1995: THE OKLAHOMA CITY BOMBING At 9:02 a.m., just as the workday was starting for some 550 government employees at the Alfred P. Murrah Federal Building in the center of Oklahoma City, Oklahoma, the state capital, a huge blast rent the air, an orange-red fireball rose into the sky, and the north side of the nine story building collapsed. The massive destruction was the result of the explosion of a 5,000-lb. truck bomb composed of fertilizer and chemicals that left a crater 30 ft. across and 8 ft. deep. Its toll: 168 dead—including 19 children in a day-care center in the building—and 400 injured. It was the single deadliest act of terror ever to take place on American soil.

Many citizens, mindful of an attack on New York City's World Trade Center by a group of militant Muslims in 1993, initially believed the bombing must have been the work of foreigners. But the truth was sadder: only days after the blast, federal agents charged **Timothy McVeigh** and **Terry Nichols,** two U.S. Army veterans turned right-wing extremists, with the evil deed. The duo represented a growing number of citizens who accused the Federal Government of betraying the basic rights of Americans and regarded the government as an enemy of the people. The Oklahoma bombing took place on the second anniversary of a bungled federal attack on a religious cult outside Waco, Texas, led by millennialist **David Koresh** that left 70 cult members dead. In June 1997, McVeigh was convicted of murder and conspiracy and given a death sentence. Nichols was to be tried later.

MURDER BY MAIL Ted Kaczynski is arraigned as the deadly Unabomber

In 1996 police made an arrest in another case of homegrown terrorism. Over a period of 17 years a fanatical latter-day Luddite the FBI called the **Unabomber** had staged 16 brutal mail-bombings, killing three and injuring 23. On April 3, federal agents arrested Ted Kaczynski, a hermit living in a rundown Montana cabin, and charged him with being the Unabomber. ■

WAVE OF TERROR The blast of the huge homemade bomb was felt 30 miles away

"On the last day of 1954 the Dow Jones industrial average hit an all-time high of 404.39 ... a clear measure of the soaring strength of the U.S. What gave the bull market historic significance was that it symbolized the strongest possible confidence in the capitalistic system."

–TIME, JANUARY 10, 1955

BUSINESS

IN THE AGE OF HENRY FORD, THE PULSE OF THE century could be taken in revolutions per minute—and in the business world, it often seemed that there was one. As the 1900s dawned, America was still in the last stage of the industrial revolution, and the titans of business thought big, bought big, made big: in steel, in railroads, in coal and cars and trucks. But near the century's midpoint—while the great bull market of the 1950s lofted the Dow Jones average to an incredible 404 points—the industrial age gave way to the electronic information age. The pendulum swung, and now the secret was to think small. First the transistor, then the microchip, then the microprocessor became the minute dynamos that generated a powerful new era of commercial growth.

DAVID SARNOFF
JULY 23, 1951

TOM WATSON, JR.
MARCH 28, 1955

BILL GATES
JANUARY 13, 1997

" The flight was fairly routine until we reached supersonic speed. It then became a new and exhilarating sensation—like having the carpet of the world map magically moved away from you. Just 20 minutes after Venice, the heel of

THE CONCORDE
First test flight, 1975

the Italian boot had been reached. But in terms of space, the Concorde seems like a throwback to the cramped piston age. 'Mind your head,' warned the steward as I boarded. "

–TIME, FEBRUARY 2, 1976

The Mighty Bug

A Model T with a German accent, the Volkswagen "Beetle" was cheap, ugly and lovable. Despite its origin—it was commissioned by Adolf Hitler as a "people's auto"—it became the world's most widely sold car in the '50s and '60s.

1949 The first Beetles go on sale in America

GETTING IN GEAR

AUTUMN 1913: THE MOVING ASSEMBLY LINE Detroit automaker Henry Ford had been turning out his innovative Model T since 1908, but in 1913 he perfected a perhaps even more significant innovation. During the spring and summer, Ford and his chief engineers experimented with a new method of **Mass Production.** By placing the auto components to be assembled on a moving production line and radically simplifying the specific task of each worker, The Ford team accomplished a nifty trick: they accelerated the assembly process even as they lowered labor costs.

In August it required an average of 12½ man-hours to make a Model T chassis. When the chassis was placed on a moving line with workers keeping pace with it, collecting parts as needed along the way, the average number of man-hours needed to do the job fell to just below six. Assembly time was lowered even more dramatically when the chassis was placed on an elevated line that moved while the workers remained stationary.

Ford was the father of another revolution. His brilliantly simple design for the Model T put auto ownership, formerly a perquisite of the wealthy, within the reach of Everyman. America became car-crazy: roads had to be built; oil wells drilled; gas stations, motels, "tourist traps"—and **Interstate Highways**—constructed. There was no turning back.

Like Ford, the century would fall in love with speed. In 1976 the British and French would introduce the **Concorde,** and for the first time ordinary men and women broke through the sound barrier. ■

1955 The first interstate highway opens in Los Angeles

BEAT THE CLOCK By 1914 Ford could roll out a new Tin Lizzie in just 93 minutes

PURE POWER

SIGN OF THE TIMES Under the new law, Uncle Sam would now vouch for the quality of meat

JUNE 30, 1906: THE PURE FOOD AND DRUG ACT Fellow novelist Jack London called Upton Sinclair's *The Jungle* "the *Uncle Tom's Cabin* of wage-slavery." Sinclair's novel on the unhealthy practices of the meat industry led Congress to pass the Pure Food and Drug Act, inserting the Federal Government into the meat business, only six months after *The Jungle* was published.

The highly controversial action was a capstone of Progressive-era politics. At the turn of the century the long reign of unbridled laissez-faire capitalism had resulted in a marketplace dominated by a few mighty trusts. One emblematic deal: in 1901 financier **J.P. Morgan** presided over the sale of Andrew Carnegie's steel interests to a new group—U.S. Steel—that became the world's first billion-dollar corporation.

COLOSSUS U.S. Steel's Pittsburgh operations in the early 1900s

But in the first decade of the new century a coalition advocating social reform through government intervention began to put checks on the power of business. Investigative journalists set out to expose the corruption and excesses of the big trusts. Such "muckrakers" included **Ida Tarbell,** who waged a lengthy struggle to document the competition-busting practices of John D. Rockefeller's Standard Oil trust.

The progressives' radical notion that the Federal Government had a right to interfere in business to guard the public interest found its most powerful ally in President **Theodore Roosevelt**, who turned the previously little-used Sherman Antitrust Law of 1890 into a trust-busting pile driver. After taking on the railroads in 1902, Roosevelt went on to win some 40 other cases that began to restore competition to commerce. ■

The Odd Couple

UPTON SINCLAIR *claimed to be shocked by his success*

No one was more surprised by the powerful impact of *The Jungle* than its author. "I aimed for the public's heart," said Upton Sinclair, "and by accident I hit it in the stomach." The alliance between progressive journalists like Sinclair and the energetic young President, Theodore Roosevelt, was complex. When

THEODORE ROOSEVELT *tagged his era with epithets*

Roosevelt, so often an ally of the progressives, christened the most extreme of the reporters "muckrakers," the journalists adopted the name with pride. Roosevelt—the "bully pulpit" man—had a gift for the right phrase: he called the business barons "malefactors of great wealth" and the most radical of the reformers "the lunatic fringe."

"BLACK TUESDAY" Mounted police try to maintain order as panic grips a Wall Street crowd

CRASH!

OCTOBER 29, 1929: THE STOCK MARKET COLLAPSE For so many months so many people had saved money and borrowed money, and borrowed on their borrowings, to possess themselves of the little pieces of paper by virtue of which they became partners in U.S. industry. Now they were trying to get rid of them even more frantically than they had tried to get them. Stocks bought without reference to their earnings were being sold without reference to their dividends. After a week of slumping stock prices, the suspicion that there might be a panic turned to the apprehension that there *was* a panic. On Tuesday the 29th, 16,338,000 shares of U.S. Industry and Commerce were dumped as if they were so much junk. The Depression was on.

Fifty-eight years later came the century's second great stock crash; in fact, the 1987 debacle was technically greater than that of 1929. On October 19, **"Black Monday,"** the Dow Jones industrial average plunged 508 points, an incredible 22.6%. Some $500 billion in paper value, a sum then equal to the entire gross national product of France, vanished into the ether.

The second crash paralleled the first: like the roaring 1920s under business-friendly Calvin Coolidge, the '80s were boom years under Ronald Reagan, a time when fortunes were conjured out of thin air by fresh-faced traders who created nothing more than paper—gilded castles in the sky held aloft by red suspenders. Said TIME: "What crashed was more than just the market. It was the Reagan Illusion: the idea that there could be a defense buildup and tax cuts without a price, that the country could live beyond its means indefinitely." ■

OCTOBER 19, 1987 Farewell to the great yuppie market

THE QUEST FOR FUEL

MAY 26, 1908: OIL IS FOUND IN PERSIA In 1859 oil was discovered in Pennsylvania, sparking a boom that created John D. Rockefeller's mighty Standard Oil Company. Yet by the turn of the century a new power source, electricity, threatened to supplant oil's chief function, illumination. But in a remarkable historical coincidence, just as the fledgling auto industry was creating an enormous demand for oil, vast new reserves of petroleum were found in America and the Middle East.

Within years, oil—"black gold"—was one of the most precious substances on earth. The quest for "the prize," as Daniel Yergin termed it in a 1990 best seller, would shift the world's balance of power.

The need for fuel drove Winston Churchill in 1914 to nationalize Britain's oil interests in Iran; in 1942 it drove Montgomery against Rommel in the desert. It gave us the '70s heyday of the **OPEC** cartel, drove **Saddam Hussein** into Kuwait in 1990—and sent the allies against Saddam in early 1991. President George Bush, whose first job had been in the Texas oil fields, declared the U.S. must wage war in the gulf to protect its "vital interests" there.

GUSHER! Spindletop led Texas to a new destiny

The frenzy began in the early days of 1901, when prospecting wildcatters brought in the century's first dramatic oil discovery, the **Spindletop** well, outside Beaumont, Texas. It took nine days to cap the oil that surged some 200 feet in the air. Soon land prices also gushed—from $10 for one acre to as much as $900,000 an acre. As hustlers and con men perpetrated frauds on get-rich-quick dreamers, the region was christened Swindletop.

Less than a decade later, on May 26, 1908, British speculator and gold-mine millionaire **William Knox D'arcy** found a gusher in the region then known as Persia, now known as Iran. Oceans of oil lay beneath the sand. In a transformation worthy of the *Arabian Nights*, the barren deserts of the nomadic Bedouin had become—as they have remained—a flash point of global tension. ■

MODERN OASIS Oil wealth took Saudi sheiks from camels to jets in a single swift leap

"Priced at $9 billion, the Alaska oil pipeline is the most expensive privately financed construction project in history. In keeping with its grandeur and technical sophistication, it has produced unprecedented engineering, financial, environmental

THE ALASKA PIPELINE
Snaking through Eden

and legal headaches. Nevertheless, this week—nearly a decade after the project's conception and more than three years after construction started—the Alaska pipeline begins carrying its first oil through nearly 800 miles of forbidding wilderness ... passing over or under 800 streams or rivers."

–TIME, JUNE 27, 1977

MAJOR OIL FINDS

- 1901 Texas
- 1908 Persia (Iran)
- 1910 Mexico
- 1922 Venezuela
- 1930 East Texas
- 1932 Bahrain
- 1938 Kuwait
- 1948 Saudi Arabia
- 1968 Alaska
- 1969 North Sea

"He had always been a good family man—even his most unrelenting enemies would admit that—and so his wife Josephine began to fret when he did not return home as planned last Wednesday after lunch. [The next day] the

JIMMY HOFFA
The mystery endures

police found his car, a dark green Pontiac hardtop, 15 miles northwest of Detroit. But there was no sign of Jimmy Hoffa, 62, the stubby, cocky, belligerent figure who was as tough as any truck driver on the road and who loved to wield the power of the Teamsters, the strongest and most feared labor union in the U.S."

–TIME, AUGUST 11, 1975

LABOR MILESTONES

- 1902 Coalworkers win with Roosevelt's aid
- 1909-14 Garment workers gain rights
- 1913-14 Massacres of mineworkers in West Virginia and Colorado
- 1937 Workers finally unionize Big Steel
- 1970 Postal workers win concessions

BATTLE IN FLINT
Picketers smash the windows of GM's Chevrolet motor plant

SHOWDOWN IN MICHIGAN

DECEMBER 28, 1936: LABOR'S TRIUMPH OVER GM Long frustrated in winning union recognition, workers at General Motors turned to a new tactic: a sit-down strike. Taking over GM plants, they began a struggle that would ultimately close 28 factories and idle some 93,000 of GM's 135,000 production workers. "On the battle's outcome," said TIME, "hung the whole future of U.S. industrial relations." Forty-four days later, General Motors conceded defeat, signaling a new era of power for the unions.

The first part of the century was the heroic era of the labor movement. When 150,000 anthracite-coal miners struck in 1902, Theodore Roosevelt intervened on the side of the miners, forcing arbitration. Later, galvanized by the deadly fire at the **Triangle Shirtwaist Factory** in New York City and led by idealistic outfits like the **Wobblies,** urban workers staged enormous and effective strikes. But union power faded in the boom times of the '20s.

Unions grew more powerful under the labor-friendly New Deal, but after World War II Harry Truman clashed time and again with the headstrong leader of the United Mine Workers, **John L. Lewis.** In 1952 Truman seized the nation's steel mills when workers struck, but the Supreme Court ruled the action unconstitutional.

In the 1960s **Jimmy Hoffa,** a leader TIME described as having "incredibly concentrated will power and vitality," built the Teamsters Union into the nation's most powerful, but his association with organized crime permanently tarnished labor's image. By 1981, when Ronald Reagan's firing of **Air-Traffic Controllers** who walked off the job was supported by most Americans, the mighty engine of union power seemed out of gas. ■

MARCH 25, 1911 The Triangle Shirtwaist fire killed 146

EMPIRES OF THE AIRWAVES

JULY 1, 1941: THE FIRST NETWORK TV BROADCASTS Under the auspices of the Federal Communications Commission, NBC and CBS began beaming the first commercial television programs on the same day. The new medium was long anticipated: RCA had thrilled visitors to the New York World's Fair of 1939 with its display of TV technology. TIME's opinion of the new medium: "The chief drawback is that the screen is so small that objects in the background are all but subvisible. There is practically nothing but drawbacks to the live programs. The actors, who tan under the Birdseye lights, must work at close quarters to stay within the camera's focus. They seem to have to compensate for physical restriction by over-emoting."

SCOOP! CNN covers the Gulf War, live from Baghdad

TIME and its readers understood that the new medium would evolve, for they had already lived through the first great broadcast marvel of the century, radio. When radio stations **KDKA** in Pittsburgh and **WWJ** in Detroit began the era of commercial broadcasting on November 2, 1920, the growth of radio, shepherded by visionary David Sarnoff at RCA, was phenomenal: inexpensive sets could soon be found in almost every home. Though the first TV newscast was a CBS report on December 7, 1941, of the Japanese raid on Pearl Harbor, Americans followed World War II on their radios, via the accounts of legendary journalists like **Edward R. Murrow.** Later he and fellow WW II radio veterans like **Walter Cronkite** would bring their authority to television news.

Through the 1950s and '60s commercial TV was dominated by CBS, NBC and ABC. Their first competition arose from cable systems like **HBO,** which debuted in 1972. On June 1, 1980, Ted Turner launched his 24-hour Cable News Network; in 1991 **CNN** scooped the world with its live broadcasts from Baghdad as the Gulf War began. ■

"ON THE AIR" Laura Suarez in an early live NBC drama, *When They Play a Waltz*

"The night attack has started, and I am with a fire brigade in a sandbag crow's nest on top of a tall building near the Thames.' So somberly, portentously, Edward R. Murrow began a broadcast of the London blitz in the early days of

EDWARD R. MURROW
Giving war a voice

World War II. To listeners in the U.S., his resonant, sepulchral voice came to convey the grim reality of war. Murrow followed Londoners on their way to air-raid shelters and caught their footsteps on his mike; he joined R.A.F. pilots on their raids over Germany and described the nightmarish rainbow of flak and fire."

—TIME, MAY 7, 1965

INSIDE BIG BLUE
IBM's punch-card press assembly line in 1955

“The enduring American love affairs with the automobile and the television set are now being transformed into a giddy passion for the personal computer. Thanks to the transistor and the silicon chip, the computer has been reduced so dramatically in both bulk and price that it is accessible to millions. It is the end result of a technological revolution that has been in the making for four decades and is now hitting home. In 1982 a cascade of computers beeped and blipped their way into the American office, the American school,

PERSONAL COMPUTER
Machine of the Year 1982

the American home. The “information revolution” that futurists have long predicted has arrived, bringing with it the promise of dramatic changes in the way people live and work, perhaps even in the way they think. America will never be the same. In a larger perspective, the entire world will never be the same.”

–TIME, JANUARY 3, 1983

THINKING MACHINES

MARCH 1955: THE FIRST OFFICE COMPUTERS The century marched in to the clank of steel; it will surf out on a silicon chip. America's transition from industrial society to information society neatly divides at mid-century: Remington Rand delivered its first UNIVAC machine to the U.S. Census Bureau in 1951; IBM installed its first mainframe, the 702, in the head office of chemical giant Monsanto in 1955. These were the bulky harbingers of the information age, an age that would transform business practices—and personal lives—everywhere.

Though IBM—International Business Machines—began by playing catch-up to Remington Rand, "Big Blue" was the better marketer. By the 1960s its mainframes seemed to be in most offices in America and its buttoned-up style was the model for corporate culture. But IBM failed to anticipate the promise of the personal computer. When **Apple** released its pioneering Apple II in 1977, IBM was left behind.

Again, Big Blue caught up, pushing its own version of the PC into offices and homes. But IBM failed to secure exclusive rights from supplier **Microsoft** to MS-DOS, the operating system that ran its PC. The young company headed by Bill Gates and Paul Allen sold MS-DOS to IBM's competitors, and soon dominated the industry.

The third wave in America's rush to a wired society was the unexpectedly rapid widespread adoption of the **Internet** and online services in the '90s. A crystallizing moment in "Internet fever" occurred in August 1995, when **Netscape,** the maker of the most popular Internet browser, first offered its stock to the public. Shares in the fledgling company opened at $14; within days they stood at $172. As gushers go, Netscape was a silicon Spindletop. ■

HACKERS Gates, bottom left, and Microsoft staff, 1975

FAST FOOD, QUICK

MAY 6, 1955: McDONALD'S INVADES AMERICA Impressed by a small chain of drive-in restaurants in California run by brothers Richard and Maurice McDonald, milk shake-mixer salesman Ray Kroc bought the rights to franchise their business, and soon Golden Arches covered the land. Kroc—the "pharaoh of fast food" to TIME—took a familiar American institution, the greasy-spoon hamburger joint, and transformed it into a radically different though still quintessentially American operation: a computerized, standardized, premeasured, superclean production machine backed by a relentless marketing blitz. The franchising of America had begun. ▶

AND—IT'S CHEAP! Ray Kroc's mantra for fast-food success: QSC—quality, service and cleanliness

CREDIT

Revolution on Main Street

1950: CREDIT CARD
Frank X. McNamara introduced the modern credit card—"plastic money"—with his new creation, the Diner's Club

1955: POCKET RADIO
Bell Telephone invented the transistor, but the Japanese first capitalized on its potential. Sony's TR-55 sounded the starting gun in the race to miniaturize technology

1900: BROWNIE CAMERA
George Eastman had simplified picture taking with his box camera of 1888. Now, with the $1 Brownie, the father of the snapshot put cameras in the hands of children

1946: LEVITTOWN
Few Americans lived in suburbs before William Levitt began to build his development on Long Island, but when Levitt's supply of inexpensive units met the demand of house-hungry World War II veterans, the modern 'burb was born

San Francisco

ONE-TWO PUNCH
Many buildings withstood the quake, only to succumb to fire

Earthquake

APRIL 18, 1906

The earthquake—an 8.3 on the Richter scale—came at 5:12 a.m. in two waves. The first lasted 40 seconds, the second 25 seconds. But the fires they sparked burned for three full days,

FIRE! 28,000 buildings burned to the ground

devouring four square miles of mostly wooden structures dating from the city's days as a gold-rush boom town. More than half of the 400,000 residents were homeless; 700 were dead. The undaunted residents dusted themselves off, and built 20,000 new homes in only three years. ■

The Titanic

APRIL 14, 1912

Perhaps because it easily bears such a heavy load of symbolism, the loss of the British ocean liner *Titanic* on its maiden voyage has become the archetypal tragedy of the century. The opulent ship was promoted over and over as "unsinkable." But sink it did—only to become an emblem of the hubris of the early 1900s, when it seemed there were no barriers that could not be broken by mammoth outlays of technology, cash and hype. In this view, its swift destruction—prefiguring the *Hindenburg* and *Challenger* tragedies—is a lesson about man's limitations in the face of nature.

The ship, speeding to set a new record for the North Atlantic crossing, collided with an iceberg shortly before midnight on April 14; it broke apart and sank just over two hours later. There was little time to evacuate the vessel, and not enough lifeboats for all: as its orchestra played, some 1,500 of the more than 2,200 passengers and crew aboard went down with the ship—including Captain E.J. Smith.

Scientists who made repeated dives to the remains of the *Titanic* in 1996 discovered that the iceberg damage—far from being the mighty gash some had suspected—amounted to no more than six small punctures, fatally located in a 12-sq.-ft. area of the ship's starboard watertight holds. ■

CRACK-UP
The ship was a "luxury liner"—but it didn't carry enough lifeboats

BON VOYAGE! The *Titanic* in Liverpool, bound for Ireland and the U.S.

The Influenza Epidemic

Children wore camphor-filled bags to ward off the deadly virus

MARCH 1918

By the end of the century it had almost been forgotten. But the devastating influenza epidemic of 1918-19 was the most wide-ranging disaster of the century, crossing national barriers to infect some 1 billion people and claim more than 20 million victims in less than a single year.

Because Spain was especially hard hit, the disease came to be called the "Spanish flu," although the virus seems to have first appeared at Fort Riley, Kansas, in March 1918. American soldiers landing in France to fight in World War I spread the disease to Europe; homeward-bound soldiers and sailors later sent it roaring throughout the world. Doctors could offer no cure. By the time the flu vanished—as quickly as it had appeared—12 million in India and an estimated 550,000 in America had perished.

In 1997 U.S. scientists obtained genetic material of the Spanish flu from a victim's lung tissue that had been preserved by U.S. Army doctors. The modern team concluded that the flu passed from birds to pigs to humans. They also believe the strain was unusually deadly because it rapidly filled victims' lungs with fluids, causing them to die "as if they had drowned." Their interest was more than historical: today's epidemiologists consider the outbreak of a similarly deadly flu to be highly probable. ■

PUBLIC ENEMY NO. 1 Seattle police donned protective face masks

MAY 6, 1937

More deadly catastrophes have followed, but the crash of the German zeppelin *Hindenburg* remains the most memorable aviation disaster of the century. The spectacular incineration of the airship was the first great tragedy to be recorded by the news media, then relived in all its urgency by a huge audience.

Scores of newsreel and still cameras captured the incredible visual spectacle of the 803-ft. ship's explosion and collapse. Even more arresting was the radio reporting of announcer Herbert Morrison, whose story was not being broadcast, but was being recorded for later replay. When Morrison interrupted his account of the routine landing by screaming into the microphone ("It's burst into flame!"), and then began to cry ("Oh, the humanity!"), those listening later thrilled to a new experience: the galvanizing jolt of history captured with its shocking immediacy intact.

The final tally in the crash: 15 passengers dead, 20 crew members dead, one member of the ground crew dead. Miraculously, 62 of those on board survived. Investigators found that the explosion was caused when atmospheric electricity ignited a leak of the highly flammable hydrogen that gave the ship its loft. The days of the giant airships died with the *Hindenburg*. ■

"Silhouetted by the holocaust, passengers began dropping out of the windows like peas from a colander. From the control cabin swarmed officers and crew. Struggling figures emerged from the blazing hulk, stumbled, rose, fell again in fiery suffocation or from broken legs, shock, concussion. Down on the slowest ones then smashed the enormous incandescent mass in a blazing blizzard of fabric, crashing girders, melted duralumin."

–TIME, MAY 17, 1937

The Hindenburg

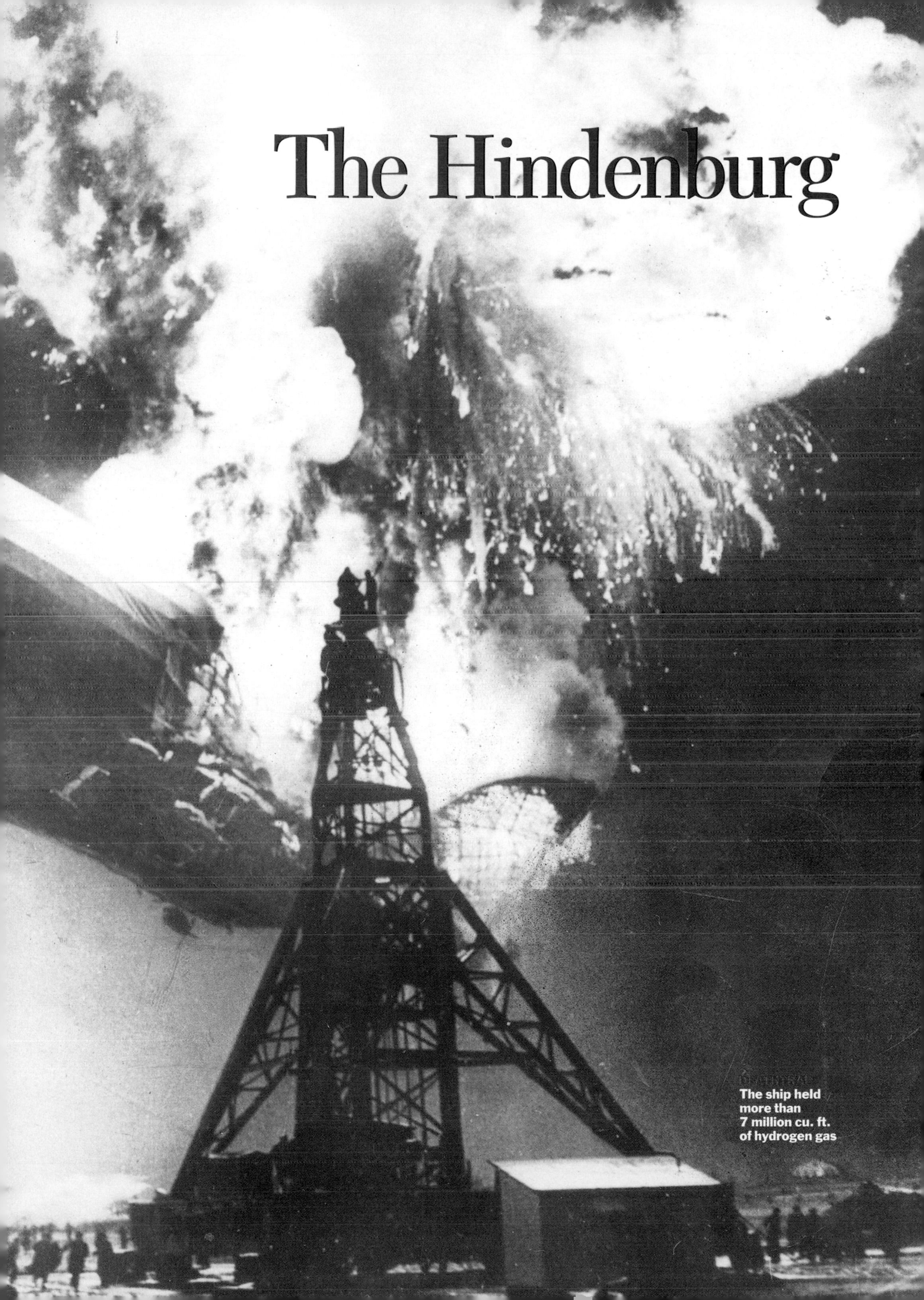

The ship held more than 7 million cu. ft. of hydrogen gas

The Challenger

“Is God dead? The three words represent a summons to reflect on the meaning of existence. No longer is the question the taunting jest of skeptics for whom unbelief is the test of wisdom. Even within Christianity, now confidently renewing itself in spirit as well as form, a small band of radical theologians has seriously argued that the churches must accept the fact of God’s death, and get along without him.”

–TIME, APRIL 8, 1966

“The loss of the shuttle inflicted upon Americans the purest pain that they have collectively felt in years. It was pain uncomplicated by the divisions—political, racial, moral—that usually beset American tragedies. The crew, spectacularly democratic, was the best of us. The mission seemed symbolically immaculate, the farthest reach of a perfectly American ambition to cross frontiers. And it simply vanished in the air.”

—TIME, FEBRUARY 10, 1986

LOST IN SPACE
The $1.2 billion *Challenger* was lifting off on its 10th mission

JANUARY 28, 1986

Americans had soared into space 55 times over 25 years, and their safe return had come to be taken for granted. An age when most any one could go along for a safe ride seemed imminent. Christa McAuliffe, an ebullient high school teacher from New Hampshire and the first ordinary citizen to be shot into space, was the vibrant symbol of this amazing new era of space for Everyman.

The era lasted only 73 seconds. For the millions of Americans watching the launch on television, disbelief turned to horror as McAuliffe, six fellow astronauts and the space shuttle *Challenger* disappeared in a fireball nine miles above the Atlantic Ocean just after lift-off. Again and again Americans watched replays of the explosion. Communal witnesses to tragedy, they were bound by a nightmarish image destined to linger in the nation's shared consciousness.

Shuttle flights were suspended until 1988; a government commission ultimately blamed the National Air and Space Administration for launching the shuttle in unusually cold weather, despite fears that a crucial set of gaskets in the rocket boosters, the O-rings, might freeze and weaken at low temperatures. The O-rings did fail, releasing a flame that ignited the rocket's main fuel tank—and doomed the mission. ■

O

ONE OF TIME'S MOST NOTED covers posed a question whose three words summed up a century so cut loose from the certainties of the past that even the most basic beliefs no longer applied. The concentration camps, the atom bomb, the "war to end all wars" that only begot a larger war—all conspired to undermine man's faith in God and in himself. And as old social models were questioned or simply cast aside, revolutions in consciousness brought revolution to Main Street. Across America people marched for change: for women's suffrage, for equal civil rights, for—and against—the legality of abortion, for the health of our imperiled planet.

SOCIETY

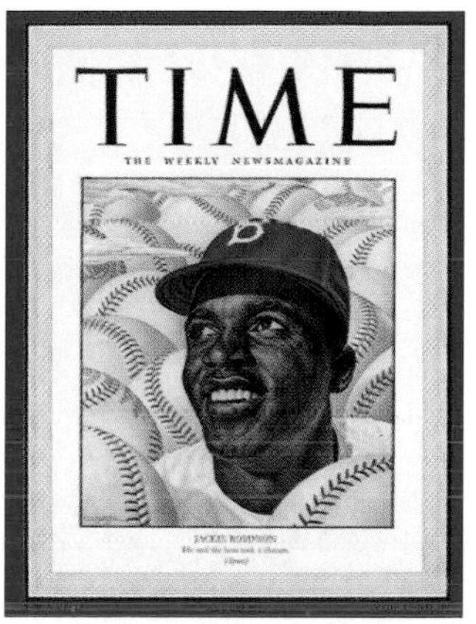

JACKIE ROBINSON
SEPTEMBER 22, 1947

POPE JOHN XXIII
JANUARY 4, 1963

ENDANGERED EARTH
JANUARY 2, 1989

THE GREAT MIGRATION

SUMMER 1907: HIGH TIDE OF IMMIGRATION Between Napoleon's defeat at Waterloo in 1815 and the onset of World War I in 1914, more than 30 million Europeans left their homes to settle in the U.S.—by far the greatest mass migration in human history. The peak year of the century-long influx came in 1907, when more than 1.2 million immigrants arrived in the New World. In contrast to the great waves of Northern European immigrants of the 19th century—Scandinavians, Germans and Irish—most of these new Americans were from Eastern and Southern Europe: Italians, Russian Jews, Poles and Greeks. Like their predecessors, they were mostly peasants, but they faced a different prospect in the U.S: the era of frontier settlement was ending.

After processing at **Ellis Island** in Upper New York Bay or at other immigration centers, millions of these rural folk found themselves confined to the mean streets of urban ghettos, like Manhattan's festering Lower East Side, working at menial jobs and crammed into narrow railroad flats without heat or privacy.

NO! Students fight Proposition 187

The nativist sentiment that foreigners are somehow inferior to the American-born may be the nation's oldest and most persistent bias. In 1924 the grandsons and granddaughters of the 18th century immigrants established a quota system based on **"national origins"** that mandated increased immigration from Northern Europe rather than from Asia and Southern Europe. The restrictive system survived until 1965.

Late in the century a flood of illegal immigrants crossed the borders of California and Texas, creating resentment and imposing heavy burdens on the states. In 1994 California voters gave strong approval to **Proposition 187,** restricting the state services provided to illegal immigrants. ■

STARTING OVER
A mother and child from Eastern Europe at Ellis Island

“Ronald Reagan lived up to a campaign pledge last week, and the nation cheered. His nomination of Sandra Day O'Connor, 51, a judge in the Arizona State Court of Appeals, to the U.S. Supreme Court, was a stunning break with tradition. In its 191-year history,

SANDRA DAY O'CONNOR
With Warren Burger

101 judges have served on the highest court; all have been men. By giving the brethren a sister, Reagan provided a powerful push forward in the shamefully long and needlessly tortuous march of women toward full equality in American society.”

–TIME, JULY 20, 1981

MILESTONES OF WOMEN'S HISTORY

- 1920 19th Amend ment gives women vote
- 1923 Equal Rights Amendment is proposed
- 1966 NOW is founded
- 1972 *Ms.* magazine
- 1977 Major women's conference in Houston
- 1984 Ferraro runs for Vice President

LONG MARCH TO EQUALITY

AUGUST 1920: WOMEN GET THE VOTE

It took decades of organized effort by women suffragists before the U.S. Constitution finally welcomed both genders at the polls. The required two-thirds of the states ratified the 19th Amendment just in time for women to vote in the presidential election of 1920. The victory concluded a crusade that began in 1848, when pioneer feminists **Elizabeth Cady Stanton** and **Lucretia Mott** organized the Seneca Falls Convention to push for women's rights. Long divided by infighting, the suffrage movement was finally united in 1890 under the banner of the National American Woman Suffrage Association, which waged a vigorous campaign for the amendment. Now enfranchised, the association evolved into the League of Women Voters, which still plays a significant role in the U.S. electoral process.

World War II propelled many women out of the home and into the work force, but during the staid, pacific 1950s, the role of suburban mother became the ideal, as critiqued by **Betty Friedan** in her groundbreaking 1963 book, *The Feminine Mystique*. The activist and writer argued that American society frustrated many of its most talented women by confining them to a narrowly defined set of roles as wife and mother.

Friedan and others founded the National Organization for Women in 1966 to lobby for women's rights. The movement accelerated in 1972, when journalist **Gloria Steinem** founded *Ms.*, a magazine devoted to the cause. Slowly, doors began to open. As TIME noted in 1984, "In 1970, only 699 women graduated from U.S. medical schools and 801 from law schools; just over a decade later, there were 3,833 graduating from medical schools and 11,768 from law schools." In other signs of change, in 1981 **Sandra Day O'Connor** was named to the U.S. Supreme Court, and in 1984 **Geraldine Ferraro** ran on the Democratic national ticket. ■

GLORIA STEINEM That's *Ms.*, not Miss

VICTORY! Women and girls rejoice in their hard-won voting rights

SOCIETY

DRY SEASON

JANUARY 1920: PROHIBITION TAKES EFFECT Herbert Hoover called it the "noble experiment," but the prohibition of the manufacture, sale, distribution and consumption of alcohol that was written into the U.S. Constitution as the 18th Amendment had an ignoble effect: it led many Americans to break the law, and it encouraged the formation of the crime syndicates that are its enduring legacy. Prohibition gave alcohol the cachet of forbidden fruit, and the roar in the Roaring Twenties was fueled by bootleg gin, supplied by organized crime and consumed in "speakeasies" under the lenient eyes of a police force corrupted by bribery.

1933 Hollywood stars raise a glass to toast repeal

Prohibition was the final triumph of the temperance movement, which flourished in the Midwest and South and was associated with Fundamentalist Christianity. Under pressure from such well-intentioned do-gooders as the Women's Christian Temperance Union and **Carry Nation's** militant Anti-Saloon League, state after state went "dry." In 1917 Congress passed the 18th Amendment and submitted it to the states for ratification; by 1919 a majority had done so, and by 1920 Prohibition was the law of the land.

In the popular mind, the 1920s remain a carefree time of flappers and jalopies, gin and jazz. But the permanent legacy of Prohibition is organized crime. In his heyday, Chicago's **Al Capone** bossed a private army of some 700 gangsters and made $100,000 a week; he graduated from running whiskey to take over the city's gambling and prostitution rackets. As rival gangs vied for turf, Chicago suffered hundreds of mob killings, though not all were as shameless as the Capone gang's infamous **Valentine's Day Massacre,** a deed TIME described as "the Austerlitz of gang killings." ■

ROLL OUT THE . . . Barrels—some 100 kegs of seized bootleg beer are dumped by agents in 1925

"It was 10:20 o'clock on St. Valentine's morning. Chicago brimmed with sentiment and sunshine. Peaceful was even the George ('Bugs') Moran booze-peddling depot on North Clark Street, masked as a garage, where lolled six underworldlings; a seventh, in overalls, tinkered with a beer vat on a truck. Into the curb eased a car, blue and fast, like the Detective Bureau's. Through the office door strode four men. Two, in police uniforms, swung submachine guns. Two, in plain clothes, carried shotguns. Snarled orders lined the gangsters up along the north wall. Then: 'Give it to 'em!' and the garage became a thunder-box of explosions. From the four guns streamed a hundred bullets. Only eight of them reached the brick wall behind the seven targets."

—TIME, FEBRUARY 25, 1929

VALENTINE'S DAY MASSACRE
Greetings from Al Capone

“In September 1955, as the nation's children trooped back to school, [the most important change] was the astounding progress of racial desegregation. In Kansas and Oklahoma and West Virginia, white and Negro children for the first time sat together in classrooms. This vast and complex

THURGOOD MARSHALL
At center, savoring his triumph

social revolution resulted from the U.S. Supreme Court's decisions of May 17, 1954, and May 31, 1955, that segregated schools are unconstitutional. The name indelibly stamped on this victory is that of Thurgood Marshall, 47.”

–TIME, SEPTEMBER 19, 1955

CIVIL RIGHTS MILESTONES

- 1947 Jackie Robinson integrates baseball
- 1954 Supreme Court desegregates schools
- 1955 M.L. King leads Montgomery bus boycott
- 1957 U.S. integrates Little Rock schools
- 1961 “Freedom Riders” stage protests

A WHOLE NEW BALL GAME

APRIL 15, 1947: JACKIE ROBINSON JOINS THE DODGERS Branch Rickey, owner of the Brooklyn Dodgers and the smartest man in major league baseball, had looked hard and waited long to find a black ballplayer who not only could represent his race proudly in the long-segregated world of America's "national pastime" but also could help the Dodgers win games. In 1945 he found his man: **Jackie Robinson**, a 26-year-old former star athlete for UCLA. Rickey scouted Robinson until he knew everything about him—and until Rickey was convinced the young man could handle the vituperation that was sure to come his way as the first black to break baseball's color barrier.

Wisely, Rickey chose to prepare Robinson with a warm-up season on the Dodgers' farm team in Montreal. He was booed in Baltimore, Maryland, and a rival team once let out a black cat from their dugout as he walked to bat, but the second baseman led the league in hitting. Montreal won the pennant—and Robinson was ready for the majors.

Speedy and skillful on the diamond, proud yet graceful under the pressure of bigotry, Robinson won over his teammates, then the local fans and finally most of the nation. His courage—and Rickey's vision—jump-started the movement for black civil rights in the U.S., a movement that gathered increasing momentum with President Harry Truman's 1948 order to integrate the armed forces; with the 1954 Supreme Court decision against segregated schools in *Brown v. Board of Education;* and with the successful 1955 bus boycott in Montgomery, Alabama, which was sparked by **Rosa Parks** and led by the young Dr. Martin Luther King Jr. ■

ROSA PARKS Changed history—by not changing seats

LOCAL HERO **Many greeted Robinson with taunts—but not these young fans**

COMMON CAUSE Large numbers of whites joined blacks to demand equal rights for all

DREAM TEAM

AUGUST 28, 1963: THE MARCH ON WASHINGTON With some 200,000 people participating, it was the largest civil rights demonstration in history—and a triumph. "We subpoenaed the conscience of the nation," said the Rev. Martin Luther King Jr., the man whose oratory made the day memorable.

The short march from the Washington Monument to the Lincoln Memorial featured no brass bands, little shouting or singing. Instead, for more than 1½ hours, there was the sound of thousands of feet shuffling toward the great, brooding statue of Lincoln. At the memorial, the first order of business was entertainment. Folk singers **Joan Baez** and **Bob Dylan** warbled; actors **Charlton Heston** and **Marlon Brando** made appearances. Then speaker followed speaker to the podium. Each was scheduled to talk for four minutes. Each spoke longer. The massive crowd became restless.

BIRMINGHAM, 1963 Police brutality shocked America

But the introduction of the last speaker, Dr. King, was drowned out by roaring cheers. He had led the spring protests earlier in the year in Birmingham, Alabama, when white police brutality had galvanized the nation. Now King's Southern-style preaching captivated his audience—and when he came to the end of his prepared text, he swept right on in an exhibition of impromptu oratory that was catching, dramatic, inspirational. "I have a dream!" King cried. The crowd began cheering as he poured out a litany of racial unity, concluding, "I have a dream that my four little children will one day live in a nation where they will not be judged by the color of their skin but by the content of their character." After the speech the marchers quickly left town. It was a quiet night in Washington—after a day that would never be forgotten. ■

"Little Rock's Central High School class bell rang at 8:45—and at almost that instant a shriek went up: 'Here come the niggers!' Four Negro newsmen had foolishly approached the white crowd from the rear. It was the tinder's spark. Some 20 rednecks turned on the Negroes, began chasing them back down the block. Other whites streamed behind. One Negro decided not to run, ambled with terrifying dignity through a gauntlet of blows, kicks and curses. A cop stood on a car bumper to get a

LITTLE ROCK, 1957
Integrating the high school

better view. While the mob's attention was distracted, the nine Negro students stepped from two cars and walked slowly, calmly into the school. But the mob had discovered that it could act violently without suffering at the hands of the cops."

—TIME, OCTOBER 7, 1957

A SYMBOL SLAIN

APRIL 4, 1968: THE ASSASSINATION OF MARTIN LUTHER KING JR. After a day spent planning a series of protest marches to support a strike by predominantly black garbage collectors in Memphis, Tennessee, Dr. Martin Luther King, America's foremost proponent of civil rights, strolled onto the second-floor balcony of the Lorraine Motel and chatted with his co-workers. Then, from a window of the rooming house across the street, came a single shot. A large-caliber bullet smashed through King's neck; he was pronounced dead within the hour. His murder was the 12th major assassination in the civil rights struggle since 1963. James Earl Ray, a white man, was apprehended; he was convicted of the killing in 1969 and sentenced to 99 years in prison.

THE FIRE THIS TIME **Police on guard in Watts, July 1965**

Martin Luther King was the transcendent symbol of the civil rights movement, bridging the void between black despair and white unconcern. At the news of his murder, blacks rioted in many cities; streamers of smoke twisted among the cherry blossoms near the Lincoln Memorial, where five years earlier King had proclaimed his vision of black-and-white harmony.

The assassination of King, TIME'S Man of the Year for 1963, ended the heroic period of the civil rights movement, whose unity had suffered when angry urban blacks rioted in a number of U.S. cities, beginning with the 1965 **Watts riot** in Los Angeles. By 1968 King's nonviolent tactics seemed naive to many young African Americans, who gravitated to the teachings of **Malcolm X,** the firebrand Black Muslim who had been assassinated in 1965. ■

IN COLD BLOOD
Dr. King's aides frantically point toward the origin of the shooting

SOCIETY

FRESH BREEZE

OCTOBER 11, 1962: THE VATICAN COUNCIL

In the aftermath of World War II, the Roman Catholic Church found itself flourishing in terms of numbers, influence and respect, and yet it was a hidebound institution, controlled by a close-knit cluster of elderly Italian Cardinals, the Roman Curia, and too often engaged in fighting old battles against Protestantism and "modernism." So rigidly hierarchical was Roman Catholicism that it was known as "the U.S. Steel of churches."

All that would change with the decision by one man—the remarkably progressive Pope John XXIII—to call a great Vatican Council, only the 20th such council in the 2,000 years of Christian history. Eager to bring "fresh air" into the church, John called 2,500 of its bishops to Rome, where, over the course of three years—well past the beloved Pope's death in June, 1963—they reshaped the church and its relation to other religions.

At the council, the bishops, who had long considered Rome the sole source of authority in the Catholic world, discovered that they and not the Vatican constituted the leadership of the church. As the progressives among them realized their strength, they revolutionized their faith. The conclave, known as Vatican II, changed the liturgy of the Mass, gave the laity a bigger role in the church and tempered the authority of the Curia. Perhaps most significantly, it encouraged a new spirit of ecumenism to heal the division between Catholics and Protestants that had dissipated the Christian message for four centuries.

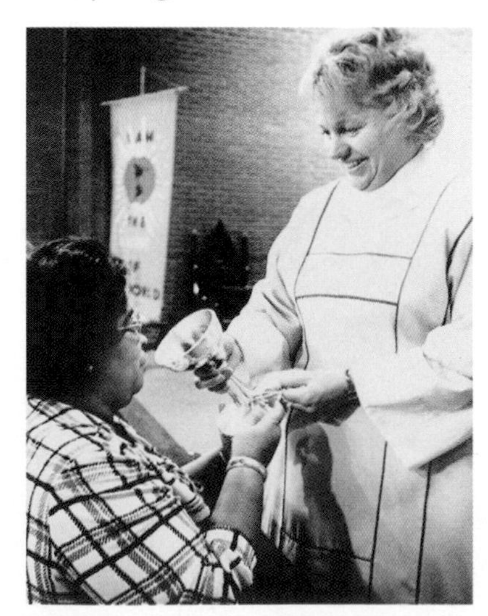

1977 The first woman Episcopal priest

Other religions also found fresh energy in the century. The evangelical Protestant tradition found new leaders in such gifted preachers as the Rev. **Billy Graham,** while Anglicans and Episcopalians welcomed women into the priesthood. Meanwhile, Islam was swept by a tide of fundamentalism that crested with the revolution in Iran led by the **Ayatullah Khomeini.** ■

A NEW AGE
An 82-year-old revolutionary—Pope John XXIII—opens the council

“Night after night in New Orleans’ 16,000-capacity Pelican stadium, this gaunt young man with the Hickey-Freeman clothes and the eagle-sharp manner is bringing men and women down from the packed stands and up the length of the baseball field to make ‘decisions for

BILLY GRAHAM
“God’s machine gun”

Christ.’ This would be news enough in that tamed but still sin-ridden city of blues and bourbon. But the flame that is searing New Orleans is also burning greater and greater swaths across the whole U.S. and around the world. Billy Graham is the best-known, most talked-about Christian leader in the world today, barring the Pope.”

–TIME, OCTOBER 25, 1954

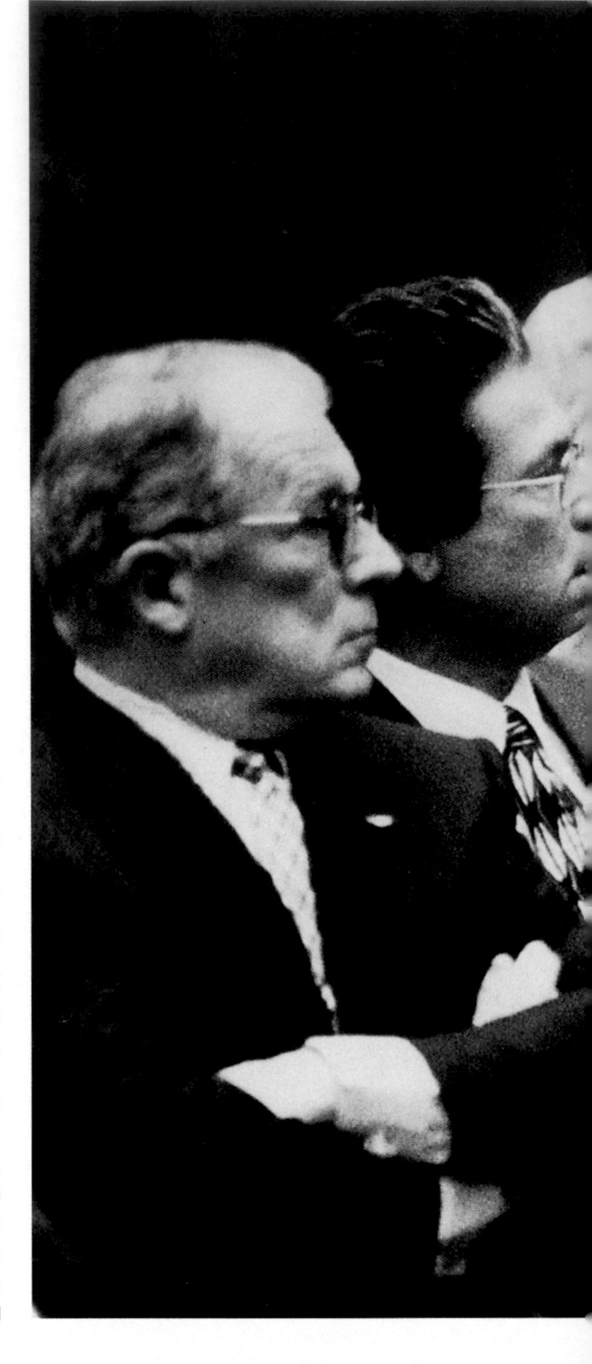

JUSTICE IN THE DOCK

OCTOBER 3, 1995: O.J. SIMPSON IS FOUND NOT GUILTY OF MURDER "We, the jury… find the defendant, Orenthal James Simpson, not guilty of the crime of murder," read the clerk in the Los Angeles courtroom. With those words, the end came at last, 474 days after football hero Simpson, 48, one of America's foremost black citizens, was charged with the knifing of his estranged white wife, Nicole Brown Simpson, 35, and Ron Goldman, 25, a restaurant waiter. After the murders, a transfixed America had watched as Simpson, on the lam, cowered in his white Bronco holding a gun to his head while a football pal drove him around the L.A. freeways. But O.J. had surrendered, and his trial became a racial litmus test. Polls showed most U.S. blacks believed Simpson the victim of a racist frame-up—the angle his lawyers pitched to the mainly black jury—while most whites felt he was guilty. In a 1997 civil suit brought by the victims' parents, Simpson was found liable for wrongful death and fined $33.5 million. ■

Courtroom Milestones

SACCO AND VANZETTI Italian-American anarchists Nicola Sacco, near left, and Bartolomeo Vanzetti were executed in 1927 for a 1920 robbery and murder in Massachusetts. Their numerous sympathizers called the trial and verdict a prejudicial witch-hunt.

THE "MONKEY TRIAL In a memorable 192 courtroom duel, fundamentalist Willia Jennings Bryan, left, took on free-thinking Clarence Darrow whe John T. Scopes was tried for opposing state law by teaching Darwin's outlawed theory of evolution in Tennessee classroo

SIGH OF RELIEF
Lead defense attorney Johnnie Cochran clutches Simpson as the verdict is read

THE LINDBERGH CASE
Bruno Hauptmann, left, a German-born carpenter who insisted on his innocence, was executed in 1936 for the sensational 1932 kidnapping and murder of the 20-month-old son of pioneer aviator Charles Lindbergh and his wife, author Anne Morrow Lindbergh.

NAZI WAR CRIMINALS
In 1946 Hermann Goering, left, Rudolf Hess, right, and 22 other top Nazis were found guilty of brutal war crimes by an Allied tribunal. Goering, who received the death sentence, swallowed poison and killed himself the night before he was to hang.

“'It is better to marry than to burn,' said St. Paul. The funny thing is, advocates of same-sex marriage and their opponents concur that it is better to marry than almost anything else. They both embrace the idea that marriage is the bedrock of a stable society... The only problem is that both sides disagree vehemently on

HERE COME THE BRIDES
Should gays legally marry?

who should be allowed to take that vow. Same-sex marriage became a hot social and political issue in 1996 because of a 1993 Hawaiian supreme court ruling that denying marriage licenses to gay couples may violate the equal-protection clause in the state constitution.”

–TIME, JUNE 3, 1996

ANTAGONISTS OF ABORTION

JANUARY 22, 1973: ABORTION IS LEGALIZED Soon after her illegitimate son was born, "Jane Roe," a divorced Dallas bar waitress, put him up for adoption. At almost the same time, "Mary Doe," an Atlanta housewife, bore a child who was also promptly adopted. Both women had asked for abortions and, like thousands of others, had been turned down. Unlike most of the others, though, Roe and Doe went to court to attack the state statutes that had frustrated them. In 1973 they heard the Supreme Court read their pseudonyms into the annals of constitutional law: by a surprising majority of 7 to 2, the court ruled that every American woman had the right to an abortion during the first six months of pregnancy.

TIME, in reporting the verdict, noted that a Gallup poll indicated some 46% of Americans favored the ruling and 45% were against it, and predicted, "Such a close division of sentiment can only ensure that [the right to abortion] remains a lightning rod for national debate." Indeed, the legalization of abortion became one of the most bitterly divisive issues in U.S. history: decades after the ruling, America was split into two voluble camps—pro-life and pro-choice—and no reconciliation was in sight.

YES! A pro-choice advocate, 1991

Once highly taboo, sexuality emerged as a pivotal social issue in the 20th century. Early on, **Margaret Sanger** promoted the then radical notion of controlling pregnancy. With the 1960 debut of the birth control pill, developed by **Dr. Gregory Goodwin Pincus,** the U.S. entered what TIME would call an "erotic renaissance." Later, increasing numbers of homosexuals "came out of the closet" to declare their sexual identity and call for equal civil rights, including the right to gay marriage. ■

NO! A pro-life advocate in Kansas in 1991, 18 years after *Roe v. Wade* legalized abortion

> "There is no doubt about the impact of *Silent Spring;* it is a real shocker. Many unwary readers will be firmly convinced that most of the U.S.—with its animals, plants, soil, water and people—is already laced with poison that will soon start taking a dreadful toll, and that the only hope is to stop using chemical pesticides and let the age-old 'balance

RACHEL CARSON
Conservation's Cassandra

> of nature' take care of obnoxious insects. Scientists, physicians and other technically informed people will also be shocked by *Silent Spring*—but for a different reason. They recognize Miss Carson's skill in building her frightening case, but they consider it unfair, one-sided, hysterically overemphatic."

—TIME, SEPTEMBER 28, 1962

FOUL WATERS
Two days after the wreck, the *Exxon Valdez* was still leaking oil

ON THE ROCKS

MARCH 24, 1989: THE WRECK OF THE *EXXON VALDEZ* It was just after midnight, and confusion commanded the bridge of the giant oil supertanker *Exxon Valdez.* As the ship cruised through the pristine waters of Prince William Sound off the coast of Alaska, its captain was in his cabin, and an unqualified third mate was in charge. The ship's lookout ran into the pilothouse to report that a flashing red buoy near Bligh Reef, which should have been on the ship's port side, had been spotted on the starboard side. The Coast Guard had failed to warn the ship that it was miles off course. In his cabin, Captain Joseph Hazelwood, who later admitted he had been drinking at the time, felt the shock of his huge vessel—and his career—hitting the rocks. He bolted onto the bridge, slowed the engines and managed to keep the ship from sliding off the reef.

But the damage was done: some 11 million gallons of crude oil leaked from the ship, fouling 1,056 miles of shoreline in one of the most ecologically sensitive areas in the world and killing an estimated 580,000 birds and 5,500 otters. An army of volunteers worked to clean up the mess, but their efforts could only contain the damage. Hazelwood, who was widely reviled at the time, was acquitted in 1990 of the most damaging charges stemming from the incident, while Exxon was fined $100 million, spent some $2 billion on the ongoing cleanup and paid $5 billion in punitive damages to Alaskan fishermen.

APRIL 22, 1970 The first Earth Day

The accident was one of the worst environmental disasters of the century, but others took a greater human toll. In **Bhopal,** India, some 6,000 died when deadly gas was released from a Union Carbide pesticide plant in 1984. The 1986 meltdown in the nuclear power plant in **Chernobyl,** Ukraine, caused only 31 deaths at the time, but the rates of both cancer and birth defects in the area remain very high. ■

DISCOVERIES

Race for The Poles

Scott's ship, the *Terra Nova*, is framed by an ice cave in 1911

DECEMBER 14, 1911 In a period when polar explorers were idolized, Roald Amundsen of Norway stood at the bottom of the earth, savoring his victory over Britain's Captain Robert Scott in the race to be the first person to reach the South Pole. A month later, Scott and four companions reached the pole—only to die in a blizzard during their return. American Robert E. Peary claimed to have reached the North Pole in 1909, but many believe his reckoning was off. A rival, Dr. Frederick Cook, claimed—falsely—to have beaten Peary by a year. ■

FIRST? Did Peary hit the North Pole in 1909?

In the Tomb of Tutankhamen

NOVEMBER 25, 1922 For 15 years the British archaeologist Howard Carter searched Egypt's sere Valley of the Kings for a royal tomb that had escaped the predations of grave robbers over the millenniums. His final success came almost by accident, as members of his team chanced upon the first of a flight of 16 steps leading to the tomb of Tutankhamen, who reigned—briefly—as pharaoh in the mid-14th century B.C., dying before he was 20 years old. Upon first breaking through the sealed door of the vault and glimpsing by candlelight the objects that the 18-year-old Pharaoh might need in the afterlife, Carter gasped that he saw "wonderful things": alabaster cups for the Pharaoh's wine, bejeweled amulets to ward off evil sprits, even an ivory-inlaid wooden throne to make him feel at home.

Carter discovered greater treasures when he delved furtner into the tomb of "King Tut." What he saw was "strange animals, statues and gold—everywhere the glint of gold." Indeed, Tutankhamen lived during a blaze of pharaonic wealth and power. The most famous object from the tomb is the golden mask that covered Tutankhamen's head: its burnished golden gleam evokes a bursting inner vitality that emphatically defies mortality. ■

GOLDEN OLDIE Howard Carter removes dust from Tut's 22-lb. solid-gold mask

FACE OF THE PAST The mask is inlaid with glass

The Caves Of Lascaux

TREASURE TROVE Flint and bone tools and 16 spears were also found in the cave

SEPTEMBER 12, 1940 Four teenage boys who set out to explore a cave in central France found themselves delving not only into the earth, but deep into the past. To their "indescribable joy," the walls of the cave held a gallery of majestic renderings of animals, paintings later estimated to be some 15,000 years old. The ancient bestiary included magnificent 10 ft. high red bulls, free-floating horses and other spirited creatures, perhaps painted as ritual magic to aid the artists in hunting them.

In December 1994, three middle-aged spelunkers discovered a second trove of Cro-Magnon cave paintings, in the Ardèche region of southeastern France. Experts were electrified when carbon tests dated the images at some 30,000 years old—twice the age of those at Lascaux.

The Cro-Magnon Picassos of Ardèche and Lascaux were fairly late arrivals in the vast span of human prehistory. Far from the inarticulate Alley Oops of popular myth, they were nomadic hunter-gatherers who wore animal-skin clothing, moccasins tailored with bone needles; they made beautiful, efficient flint blades. The main technique of their art, some experts believe, involved not brushes but a kind of oral spray painting—blowing pigment dissolved in saliva on the wall. ■

HIGHER GROUND
At Camp VIII, two teams prepared for the final grueling 3,200 ft.

MAY 29, 1953

Though not a discovery in the sense of a scientific revelation, the first ascent of the earth's highest peak, 29,028-ft. Mount Everest in the Himalayas, was one of the breakthrough feats of the century. Like the shattering of the 4-min.-mile barrier in track by Roger Bannister, the conquest of the famed mountain by the New Zealander Edmund Hillary and the Sherpa Tenzing Norkay expanded our notions of what men could achieve.

By 1953, 13 expeditions had set out to conquer the mountain the Sherpas call Chomolungma; none succeeded. Fifteen climbers had died on the slopes of the mountain, including George Mallory, the man who famously claimed he wanted to climb Mount Everest "because it's there."

Hillary and Norkay were members of a large expedition led by Colonel John Hunt of the British army. Seven climbers reached Camp VIII, at 25,850 ft., and two teams were ready for the final assault. After the first team turned back, Hillary and Norkay set out, camping overnight at 27,900 ft. and reaching the peak the next morning. The magnitude of their achievement was brought to mind in May 1996, when eight climbers—equipped with far superior gear—perished on the mountain in a single day after a storm struck near the summit. ■

The Conquest Of Everest

PEAK EXPERIENCE **Tenzing, left, and Hillary toast their success**

The Army Of Statues

March 1974

Like the prehistoric paintings in the caves of Lascaux, they were discovered by amateurs rather than professional scientists. Like the treasures of Tutankhamen, they were commissioned to mark the passing of a wealthy ruler. But in its sheer immensity, the army of terra-cotta warriors unearthed in 1974 near Xian in central China was unlike any other archaeological find of the century.

The first soldier was discovered by local farmers digging a well. It was a life-size figure of a warrior, made of terra-cotta and exact in every detail. As scientists excavated the area, they were amazed to uncover an entire army of more than 7,500 clay figures. Each was individually modeled—not cast from a mold—and complete with weapons and armor. The army was even accompanied by war chariots drawn by terra-cotta horses. Originally each figure had been painted in bright colors, but the statues' finery had faded during their long interment.

The army was commissioned some 22 centuries ago to guard the royal tomb of Qin Shi Huang Di, the first emperor to unify China. Huang Di was a big thinker: it was he who began building the Great Wall. His imperial mausoleum, which the statue army encircles, has yet to be excavated. ■

BODYGUARDS The statues cover an area of some 500 acres around the imperial tomb

SPACE EXPLORATION
DECEMBER 8, 1952

THE HYDROGEN BOMB
APRIL 12, 1954

CLONED SHEEP
MARCH 10, 1997

PITY THE MAN IN THE MOON. IF HE SEEMED alarmed by man's scientific progress on TIME's 1959 cover, he wasn't alone. In this century science elbowed its way to the front lines of human endeavor, joining politics and economics as an engine of social change. Yet it often seemed that science wore two faces: it granted wonderful blessings but demanded a frightening price. The atom was smashed—and out came the Bomb. The double helix was described—and a sheep gave birth to a clone. The simplest convenience, an aerosol spray can, turned out to threaten earth's protective ozone layer. But the advances kept coming:

radar blips, microchips, even lunar trips. Ten years after that 1959 TIME cover, man planted his feet on the moon.

SCIENCE

"When the Soviet Lunik raced past the moon and free of the earth last week, it did more than win a triumph for its designers. It also marked a turning point in the multibillion-year history of the solar system. One of the sun's planets had finally evolved a living creature that could break the chains of its home gravitational field ... This startling development took place with explosive suddenness.

–TIME, JANUARY 19, 1959"

TEMPTING FATE The brothers' favorite launching spot at Kitty Hawk was a high dune called Kill Devil Hill

THE WILD BLUE YONDER

DECEMBER 17, 1903: THE FIRST AIRPLANE FLIGHT The initial manned flight in an airship lasted only 12 sec., and the airplane traveled only 120 ft. across the sand dunes near the village of Kitty Hawk, North Carolina. Before the day was over, the two brothers who had designed and built *Flyer 1,* Orville and Wilbur Wright, achieved a flight of 59 sec. that covered 852 ft. While the Wright brothers—the owners of a custom-bicycle shop in Dayton, Ohio—exulted, at least one witness was let down. A local undertaker sat nearby in a horse-drawn buggy, watching the proceedings in hopes of picking up a little business.

As boys, the Wrights had played with kites and gliders. As young men—fired by the work of **Otto Lilienthal,** a German scientist who died in 1896 while experimenting with gliders—they continued to study aerodynamics, even building their own wind tunnel to study the physics of lift. The result of their studies, *Flyer 1,* was powered by a 12-h.p. engine placed at one side of the driver's seat. Long struts supported rudders at its rear, while two skids projected out in front to prevent the plane from somersaulting on landing.

LOST Amelia Earhart in 1932, five years before her death

By 1905 the brothers had built *Flyer 3* and were sustaining flights of almost an hour. In the years that followed, the technology of flight developed rapidly—with a major boost from the adoption of flying machines as military vehicles in World War I. In peacetime, a host of barnstormers and daredevils vied to achieve various flight "firsts." As the first pilot to cross the Atlantic alone, **Charles Lindbergh** earned universal acclaim—and TIME's designation as its first Man of the Year. In 1932 **Amelia Earhart** became the first woman to duplicate his feat. But she was lost in the South Pacific in 1937 during a round-the-world flight, and her fate is perhaps the century's greatest unsolved mystery. ■

"Hard-headed U.S. men, soft-hearted U.S. women grumblingly asked when the dangerous far-flung flights of Col. Lindbergh would cease. To date he has flown to France, Belgium, England, Mexico, Canada in the interests (his) of aviation progress and the interests (governmental) of

CHARLES LINDBERGH
TIME's first Man of the Year

international goodwill. Grumblers wondered if interest accruing to the national welfare by his flights is worth the calamitous crash of principal which would accompany his death. Thought they: "He is worth keeping." One way to keep him is to keep him on the ground. Others argued that Lindbergh must fly for his life in the public eye; heroes age swiftly when seated at office desks."

—TIME, JANUARY 2, 1928

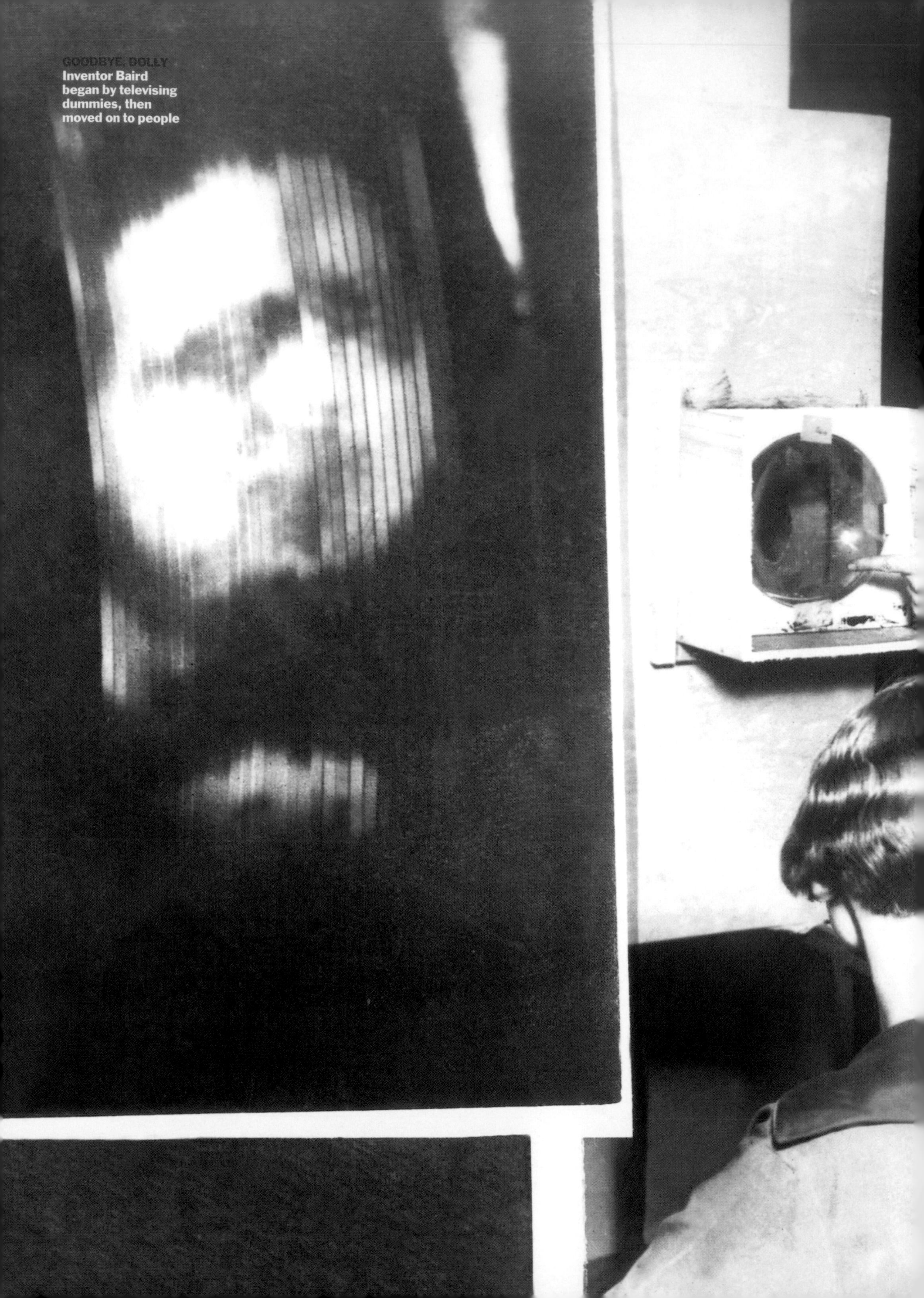

GOODBYE, DOLLY
Inventor Baird began by televising dummies, then moved on to people

ON THE AIR

OCTOBER 2, 1925: THE FIRST TELEVISED IMAGE For drama, it was less exciting than the moment in 1876 when Alexander Graham Bell accidentally sent the first telephone message ("Watson, come here, I want to see you"). But the first television transmission was odd in its own way, for the image sent by **John Logie Baird,** a Scottish inventor, was not a human face, but the head of a ventriloquist's dummy. Baird's primitive system involved a camera that scanned an object mechanically, sending a concentrated beam of light through a spinning disk with holes in it, which broke the image of the object into lines. Then a photoelectric cell converted the resulting lines into electricity, and a receiver reversed the process. But the pictures that resulted were of very poor quality.

Baird's version of the television was soon outmoded. In 1925 Russian-born U.S. physicist **Vladimir K. Zworykin** patented designs for a device he called the iconoscope, which replaced Baird's mechanical scanner with a specially treated vacuum-tube camera. In 1927 **Philo T. Farnsworth,** a young American engineer, also developed an electronic picture tube that was superior to Baird's version.

The television was the second of two great communications revolutions of the early 20th century. The first, the wireless transmission of signals by radio waves, came in the century's first year. It was precisely noon on December 12, 1901, when Italian physicist **Guglielmo Marconi** almost instantaneously received a radio signal—the letter *S* in Morse code—that had been sent by his associate John Ambrose Fleming through a grounded antenna across the Atlantic Ocean from England to Newfoundland. The radio age had begun. ■

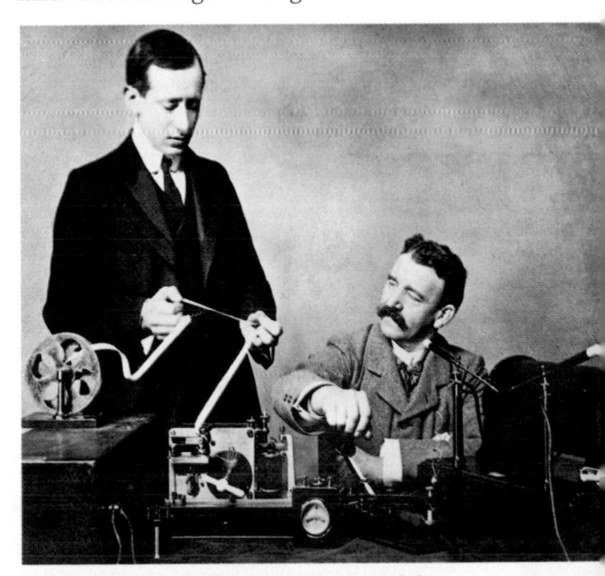

ITALIA RULES THE WAVES Marconi, at right, was a pioneer of the grounded radio antenna

SCIENCE

BOOTING UP

INSIDE THE BRAIN The gigantic ENIAC used 500 miles of wire and generated withering heat

FEBRUARY 1945: DEBUT OF THE ELECTRONIC COMPUTER After digesting a fancy dinner and a six-pack of speeches, 50 of America's most prominent scientists gathered at the University of Pennsylvania's Moore Electrical Engineering School to witness the first public demonstration of the world's latest and greatest mechanical brain—a 30-ton series of 17,468 vacuum tubes, dials and cabinets that occupied an entire room.

The enormous gadget was known as the "electronic numerical integrator and computer." Its inventors—**John W. Mauchly** and **J. Presper Eckert**—called it ENIAC. For their blue-ribbon audience, they gladly demonstrated how ENIAC could compute the trajectory of a shell in less time than it would take for the shell to reach its target. Thus, in a trice, ENIAC showed its superiority over its predecessors. Both M.I.T. and Harvard University had fast calculating machines, but they were mechanical. ENIAC was the first calculator that had no moving parts, except for the fast-flying electrons inside vacuum tubes.

No single person can be properly described as the inventor of the computer. Its development can be traced back to the "difference engine," built by the 19th century British inventor **Charles Babbage,** and the "differential analyzer," built by U.S. engineer **Vannevar Bush** in the 1930s.

In World War II British mathematician **Alan Turing** and his colleagues built an elaborate computer to crack the Germans' Enigma code. And the Hungarian-born U.S. theorist and mathematician **John von Neumann** played a key role in the development of ENIAC and its successor, EDVAC. ■

PIONEER Vannevar Bush with his differential analyzer

Small Miracles

ENIAC put computers into the electronic age, but it took two further inventions to make them faster, smaller and more affordable. The first was the transistor, a tiny device that replaced bulky vacuum tubes to amplify electronic signals. The product of years of research by William

THE FIRST TRANSISTOR *was developed by Bell Labs*

Shockley, Walter H. Brattain and John Bardeen, it was unveiled by Bell Laboratories on July 1, 1948. The second invention was the microchip, or integrated circuit, which was developed independently by inventors Jack Kilby and Robert Noyce in 1959. The microchip combined, or integrated, into a single unit the transistor and its connecting circuits, simplifying both the manufacture and operation of computers. By the 1980s, a single tiny microchip easily outpaced the mammoth ENIAC.

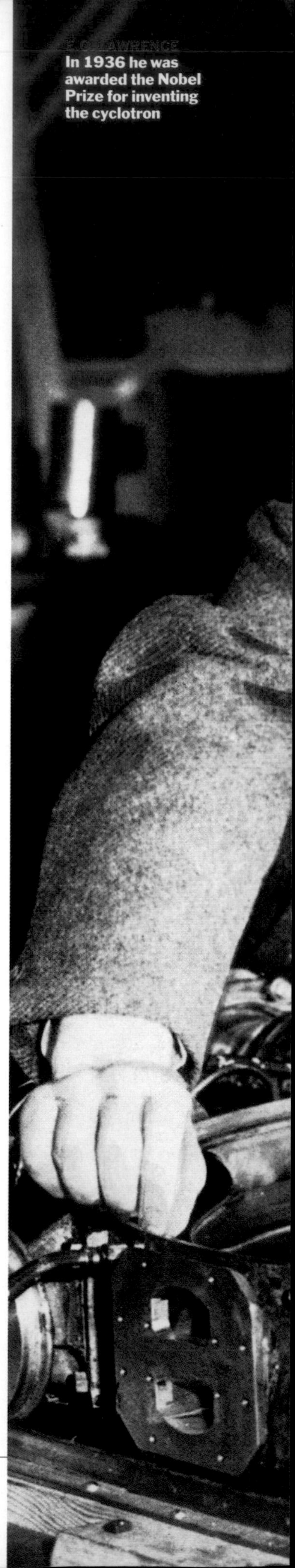

E.O. LAWRENCE In 1936 he was awarded the Nobel Prize for inventing the cyclotron

A WORLD IN A GRAIN OF SAND

DECEMBER 2, 1942: THE FIRST NUCLEAR CHAIN REACTION Fired by the Curies' discovery of radioactivity in the 1890s and dazzled by the theoretical breakthroughs of Max Planck and Albert Einstein in the first decade of the 20th century, physicists began exploring invisible realms, smashing the atom—once thought indivisible—to reveal universes within. In these tiny particles they found a lever to move the world.

In 1929 U.S. physicist **E.O. Lawrence** began building a novel device, the cyclotron, that used an electromagnet to accelerate atoms and hurl them together; it yielded a trove of new insights. By 1938 scientists had discovered nuclear fission: when uranium was bombarded with the subatomic particles called neutrons, it split apart, releasing energy. Many believed this process could create a "superbomb."

FERMI At the control panel of the nuclear pile

World War II provided the need for such a bomb, and the U.S. set up the secret Manhattan Project to build it. The first step was to create a self-sustaining nuclear chain reaction. Italian-born physicist **Enrico Fermi** and his colleagues succeeded—and gave birth to the atomic age—on a squash court under the stands of the University of Chicago's football stadium. Here they constructed the world's first uranium pile, which TIME called "a curious structure...built of dead-black graphite bricks with small cubes of uranium...embedded in some of their corners"; it was controlled by rods plated with neutron-absorbing cadmium. After one false start, the pile reached "critical mass" and sustained a nuclear chain reaction for 28 minutes, releasing more energy than was used to start it. Thirty-two months later, the *Enola Gay* released an atom bomb on Hiroshima. ■

“Through the incomparable blast and flame that will follow [next week's atom-bomb test at Bikini Atoll], there will be dimly discernible, to those who are interested in cause & effect in history, the features of a shy, almost saintly, childlike little man with the soft brown eyes, the drooping facial lines of a world-weary hound, and hair like an aurora borealis. He is Professor Albert Einstein...

ALBERT EINSTEIN
The pacifist behind the bomb

Einstein did not work on the atom bomb. When the serpent of necessity hissed, the [physicists] who bit into the apple of scientific good and evil bore different names: Dr. Enrico Fermi, Dr. J.R. Oppenheimer, Dr. Leo Szilard, *et al.* But Einstein was the father of the bomb in two important ways: 1) it was his initiative which started U.S. bomb research; 2) it was his equation ($E = mc^2$) which made the atom bomb theoretically possible.”

—TIME, JULY 1, 1946

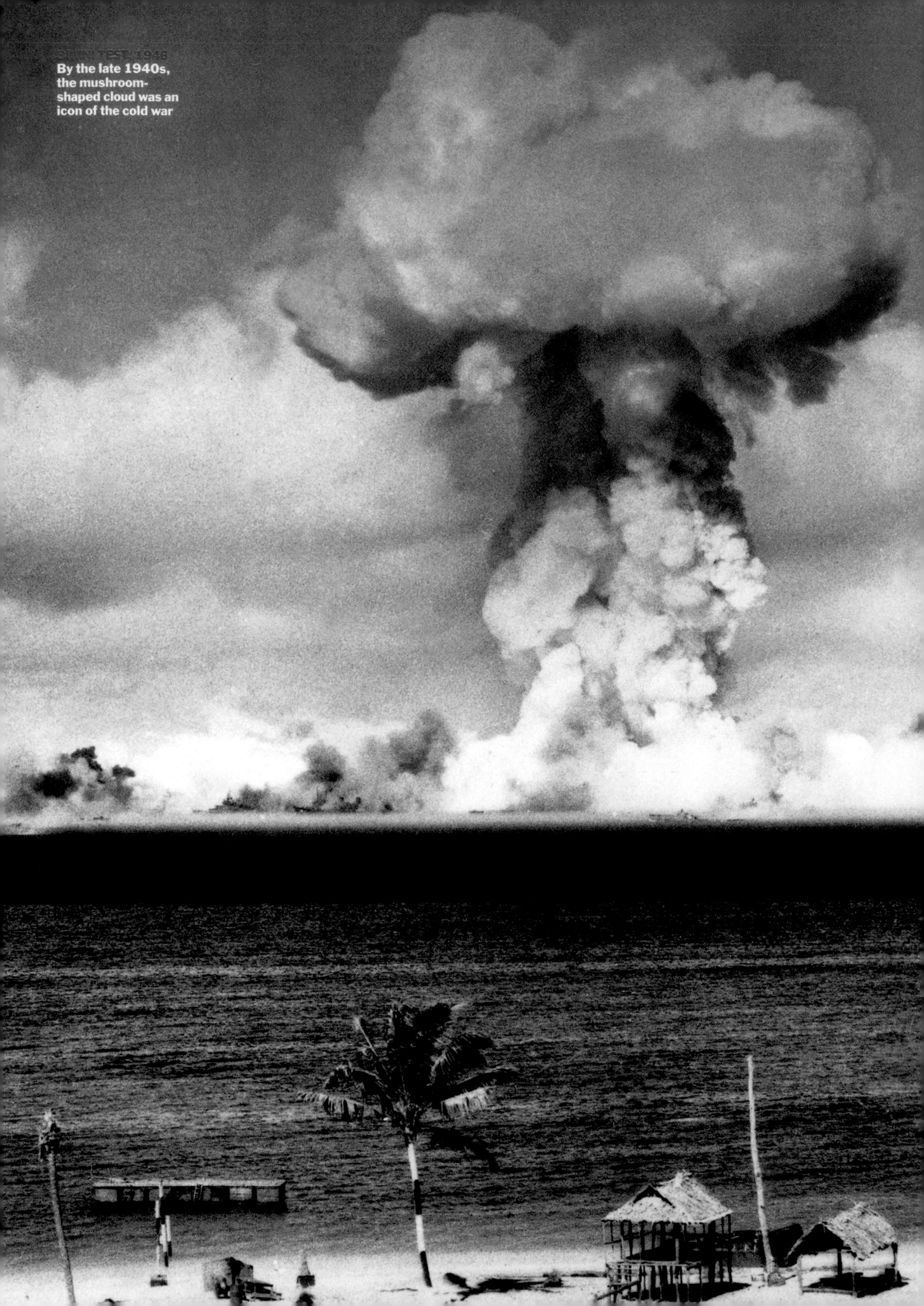

By the late 1940s, the mushroom-shaped cloud was an icon of the cold war

CULTIVATING ANNIHILATION

JULY 16, 1945: BIRTH OF THE ATOM BOMB Brigadier General Thomas F. Farrell was watching Dr. J. Robert Oppenheimer, the physicist in charge of building the atom bomb, on the day it was tested in Los Alamos, New Mexico: "He grew tenser as the last seconds ticked off. He scarcely breathed. He held onto a post to steady himself... When the announcer shouted 'Now!' and there came this tremendous burst of light, followed... by the deep-growling roar of the explosion, his face relaxed into an expression of tremendous relief." Oppenheimer later recalled that two lines of the Hindu *Bhagavad-Gita* flashed though his mind: "I am become death, the shatterer of worlds."

One month later, bombs were dropped on the Japanese cities of Hiroshima and Nagasaki—the only atom bombs ever used in wartime. The physicists who built them were heartsick: in February 1946 TIME noted, "More than six months after the first bomb flattened Hiroshima, the scientists who made it possible were a bewildered, frustrated group of men... many unhappy in what they were doing, nearly all of them worried about the future... The bomb had smashed their cloistered world as flat as Hiroshima. Disconsolately, sometimes angrily, they wandered about the ruins."

But there was no turning back. In July 1946 the U.S. began the first scientific tests of the effects of the atom bomb on minuscule **Bikini Atoll** in the Marshall Islands in the mid-Pacific. Over the course of the next 12 years, the U.S. conducted more than 60 atomic tests in the area.

The American monopoly on the atom bomb lasted for only four years: the U.S.S.R. detonated its own device in 1949, and sparked an atomic arms race. On November 1, 1952, the U.S. detonated a hydrogen bomb, driven by nuclear fusion, not fission; its principal architect was the Hungarian-born physicist **Edward Teller.** But Soviet scientists were quick to catch up; they detonated a hydrogen bomb of their own in August 1953. Oppenheimer, still plagued by guilt, had forcefully opposed the development of the hydrogen bomb. He was labeled a subversive and was stripped of his security clearance. ■

OPPENHEIMER came to believe that "physicists have known sin"

GRAVITY BUSTERS

Pioneers of the Space Age

ROBERT GODDARD
The U.S. physicist launched the world's first liquid-fueled rocket in 1926. The craft, only 4 ft. long, reached a height of 184 ft.

CHUCK YEAGER
The U.S. Air Force pilot who had the legendary "right stuff" became the first man to break the sound barrier, flying an X-1 rocket-plane in 1947.

YURI GAGARIN
In the second of the Soviets' great space breakthroughs, cosmonaut Gagarin became the first human in outer space, achieving a one-orbit flight in the *Vostok 1* on April 12, 1961.

THE *COLUMBIA*
Designed to be reusable, the U.S. shuttle was a new breed of spacecraft that was lofted into orbit by a rocket, then landed like a plane. The first flight of the shuttle *Columbia* took place in April 1981.

OCTOBER 4, 1957: THE U.S.S.R. LAUNCHES THE FIRST SATELLITE

For a small object—it weighed 184 lbs. and measured 23 in. across—Sputnik had a big impact on history. The Soviet Union not only stunned the world with its launch of the first artificial satellite; it also roared ahead in the fledgling space race, a frantic competition between the U.S.S.R. and the U.S. having as much to do with propaganda as with science. "People of the whole world are pointing to the satellite," crowed the ebullient Soviet leader **Nikita Khrushchev.** "They are saying the U.S. has been beaten." By 1958 the lagging U.S. had created NASA, the National Aeronautics and Space Administration.

Early in the century, space exploration was the stuff of pulp science fiction, and visionaries like **Robert Goddard** were often scorned. Rocket science accelerated in Nazi Germany, as physicist **Wernher von Braun's** mighty V-2 rockets battered London at the end of World War II. Von Braun came to the U.S. after the war, and he and his NASA team watched with envy as the Soviets put **Yuri Gagarin** in orbit in 1961—the first man in outer space. The U.S. quickly caught up: astronaut **John Glenn** roared into orbit early in 1962. By 1969, only 12 years after Sputnik's flight, a U.S. flag stood on the moon. ■

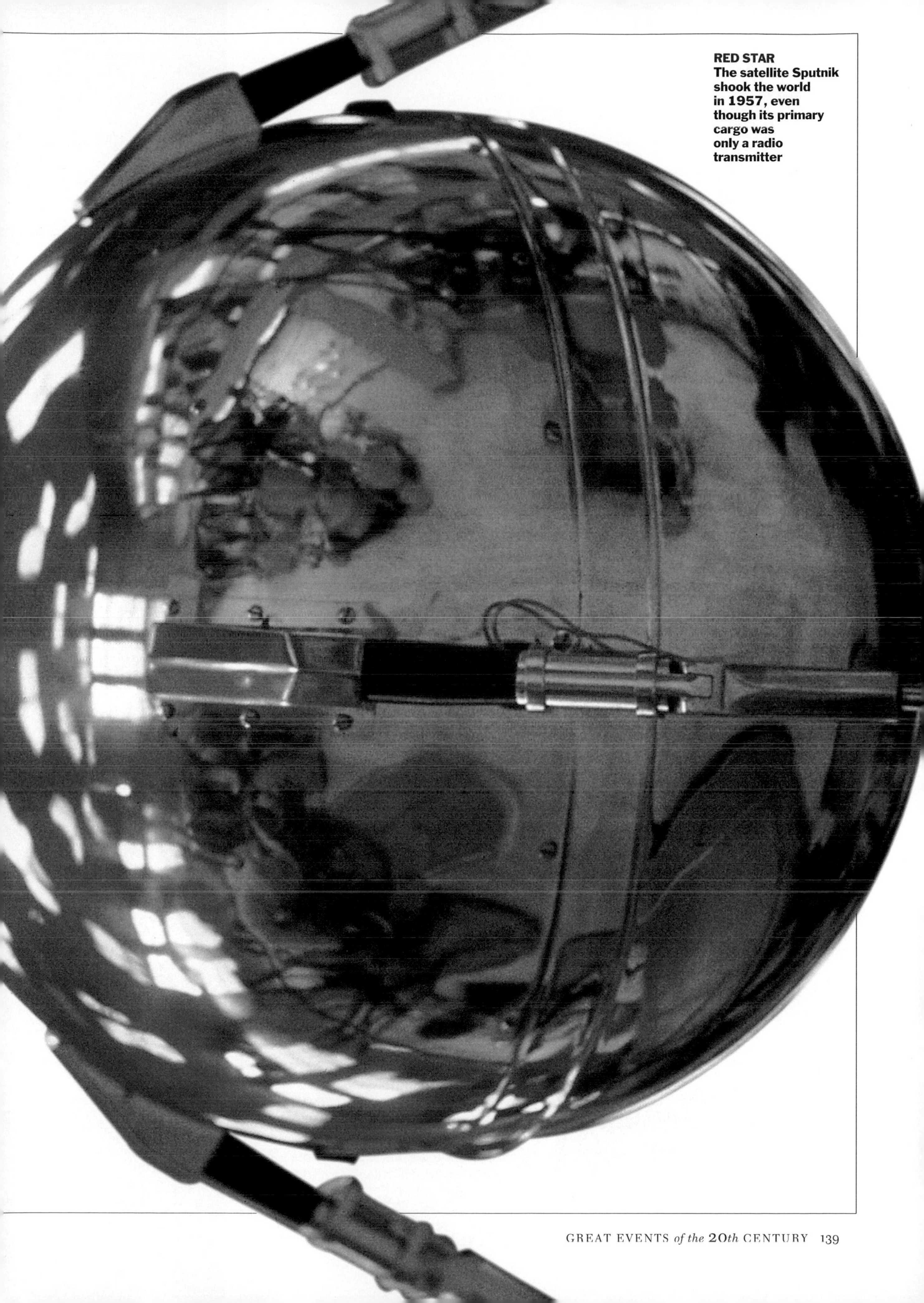

RED STAR
The satellite Sputnik shook the world in 1957, even though its primary cargo was only a radio transmitter

STRANGER IN A STRANGE LAND

JULY 20, 1969: MAN LANDS ON THE MOON The ghostly, white-clad figure slowly descended the ladder. Having reached the bottom rung, he lowered himself into the bowl-shaped footpad of *Eagle,* the spindly lunar module of Apollo 11. Then he extended his left foot, cautiously, tentatively, as if testing water in a pool—and in fact he was testing a wholly new environment for man. That groping foot, encased in a heavy multilayered boot, would remain indelible in the minds of millions who watched it on TV, a symbol of man's determination to step, and forever keep stepping, toward the unknown.

After a few short seconds—that only seemed interminable—American astronaut Neil Armstrong placed his foot firmly on the fine-grained surface of the moon. The time was exactly 10:56 p.m. Eastern. After a brief pause, the first man on the moon spoke the first words on lunar soil: "That's one small step for man, one giant leap for mankind."

With a cautious, almost shuffling gait, Armstrong began moving about in the harsh light of the lunar morning. "The surface is fine and powdery," he noted. Minutes later, he was joined by Edwin ("Buzz") Aldrin. Then, gaining confidence with every step, the two loped across the barren landscape for 2 hrs. 14 min., while the TV camera they had set up 50 ft. from *Eagle* transmitted their steps with remarkable clarity to enthralled audiences on earth, some 250,000 miles away.

Now moving in surrealistic slow motion, now bounding around the weak lunar gravity like exuberant kangaroos, they set up experiments and scooped up rocks, snapped pictures and probed the soil, clearly enjoying every minute of their stay in the moon's alien environment. Finally, after centuries of prophecies, dreams and desires, the moment had come: for the first time, man had broken his terrestrial shackles and set his feet on another world. ■

EAGLE **The landing module on the moon**

HUBBLE TROUBLE **Some of the craft's solar-energy panels were unstable and had to be replaced**

SCIENCE

ABOVE IT ALL

APRIL 25, 1990: LAUNCH OF THE HUBBLE TELESCOPE "Once aloft in the dark void of space," TIME predicted on the eve of its launching, "the Hubble Space Telescope promises a leap in astronomical observing power unlike anything since 1609, when Galileo first pointed his telescope at the heavens. As never before, astronomers have a realistic hope of seeing planets that orbit distant stars, watching tidal waves of energy swirl around black holes and spotting the birth of galaxies."

Well, that was the plan. In reality, the bus-size instrument was plagued by problems. Named for **Edwin Hubble,** the great astronomer who discovered in the 1920s that the universe is expanding, the space telescope was designed to see the cosmos 10 times as clearly as any ground-based telescope ever had, thanks to its position high above Earth's distorting atmosphere.

But once the $1.5 billion telescope had been successfully delivered into a 370-mile-high orbit by the shuttle ***Discovery,*** a major flaw was discovered in its most vital component: the 2.4-m (7.9-ft.) primary mirror, which focused light from space on an array of cameras and instruments, had been ground to the wrong curvature. The tiny error caused a major problem: images relayed by the Hubble to Earth were fuzzy. There were other troubles—faulty electronic systems, malfunctioning navigational gyroscopes, unstable solar-energy panels.

In December 1993 the National Aeronautics and Space Administration launched a mission to fix the telescope. The seven astronauts who rode the shuttle ***Endeavour*** into orbit faced the most complicated mission since the moon shots of two decades earlier. Their mandate was to sharpen the telescope's marred eyesight by fitting the instrument with corrective lenses, then tackle the Hubble's other problems. Doing the job required wrestling huge pieces of machinery into tight spaces, connecting fragile electronic equipment and making sure no loose screws damaged the delicate telescope—all while wearing puffy pressure suits and bulky gloves. The astronauts succeeded brilliantly, restoring two flawed images: the Hubble's and NASA's.

Since its repair, the Hubble has confirmed the existence of black holes, peered deep into time and captured a comet's spectacular collision with Jupiter in 1994. But it was 370 miles away from one of the most exciting space stories of the 1990s: a **rock from Mars** that may hold signs of life on other planets was discovered—not in outer space—but in Antarctica. ■

"Some 16 million years ago, a giant asteroid slammed into the dusty surface of Mars, gouging a deep crater in the planet's crust and lofting huge quantities of rock and soil into the thin Martian atmosphere. Some of the rocks, fired upward by the blast at high velocities, escaped the weak tug of Martian gravity and entered into orbits of their own around the sun. One of these Martian rocks ventured close to Earth 13,000 years ago and crashed into a sheet of blue ice in Antarctica. It lay undisturbed until scientists discovered it in 1984 in a field of jagged ice called the Allan Hills. Last week that rock—dubbed ALH84001—seized the imagination of all

MARS ROCK ALH84001
Are signs of early life inside?

mankind. This well-traveled stone appeared to have brought with it the first tangible evidence that we are not alone in the universe."

—TIME, AUGUST 19, 1996

"From the age of six months, Richard Leakey was taken on expeditions with his famous parents; he learned to recognize fossils almost before he could talk. His childhood conversations were filled with the anatomical, geological and biological jargon of anthropology. His father Louis taught

MARY AND LOUIS LEAKEY
On a dig in East Africa

"bushcraft" to Richard and his brothers by sending them out to scavenge and survive in the wild ... Richard resembles his father in more ways than he'd care to admit. Mary Leakey, a vigorous, cigar-smoking woman of 64 who still puts in eight hours a day exploring Olduvai, is also impressed. She says her son 'is rather better than Louis was.'"

–TIME, NOVEMBER 7, 1977

ON THE TRAIL OF EARLY MAN

OCTOBER 17, 1974: LUCY IS DISCOVERED She stood only 3½ ft. tall, her brain capacity was quite small, and she died at 20. But this old lady—she lived 3 million years ago—is thoroughly modern. Lucy was named after the Beatles' song *Lucy in the Sky with Diamonds;* when discovered, hers were the most intact fossilized remnants of an early hominid ever found. Unearthed by anthropologists **Donald Johanson** of the U.S. and **Maurice Taieb** of France, Lucy's skeleton showed her to be surprisingly short-legged, but proved she walked erect.

Lucy is an *Australopithecus afarensis,* one of a species whose fossils were first discovered in 1924 by South African anthropologist **Raymond Dart.** This primate had a large, apelike face, with teeth like modern man, and a brain far smaller than that of a human child yet larger than an ape's. But unlike the apes, *Australopithecus* walked erect on two legs, like the more recent *Homo erectus* species, Java man, Peking man and Neanderthal man.

In 1938 **Robert Broom** uncovered a larger type of *Australopithecus*, christened *robustus,* and in the late 1950s the married team of **Louis and Mary Leakey** began finding fossil remains similar to those of Broom at Tanzania's Olduvai Gorge and other East African sites, establishing that *Australopithecus* was as much as 2 million years old. They also found pebbles chipped to form sharp-edged implements—evidence that even so far back, some of man's ancestors could make tools. But who?

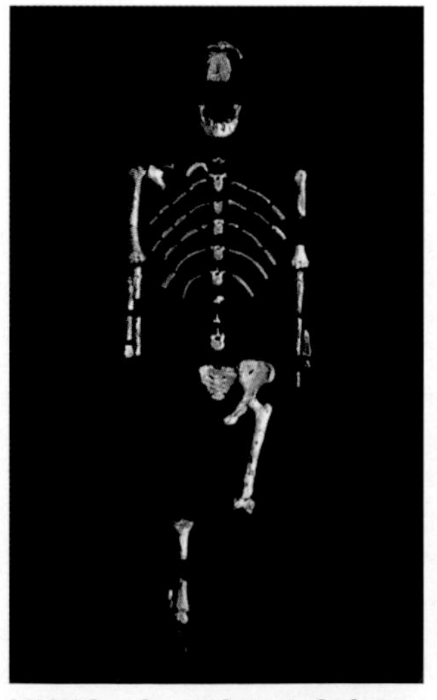

LUCY An almost intact skeleton

Later fossil finds by the Leakeys' sons—Jonathan and Richard—established the existence of a being that was more advanced than *Australopithecus:* a tool-making homonid they named *Homo habilis* ("handy man"), from whom both *Homo erectus* and *Homo sapiens (*modern man) may have descended. Richard Leakey found two skulls in the early 1970s that showed *Homo habilis* coexisted with *Australopithecus,* suggesting that the latter was not a direct ancestor of modern man but an evolutionary dead end. Yet we still love Lucy. ■

FOSSIL HUNTER
Donald Johanson with the mandible of a prehistoric horse in Ethiopia

“Jonas Edward Salk, 39, [is] an intense, single-minded medical researcher who spends his days and a large part of his nights in the University of Pittsburgh's Virus Research Lab. This spring, Dr. Salk's vision and his delicate laboratory procedures and logarithmic

DR. JONAS SALK
His vaccine crippled polio

calculations are to be put to the test. Beginning next month in the South and working North ahead of the polio season, the vaccine that Salk has devised will be shot into the arms of 500,000 to 1 million youngsters... A few months after the 1954 polio season is over, statisticians will dredge from a mountain of evidence an answer to the question, Does the Salk vaccine give effective protection against polio?”

–TIME, MARCH 29, 1954

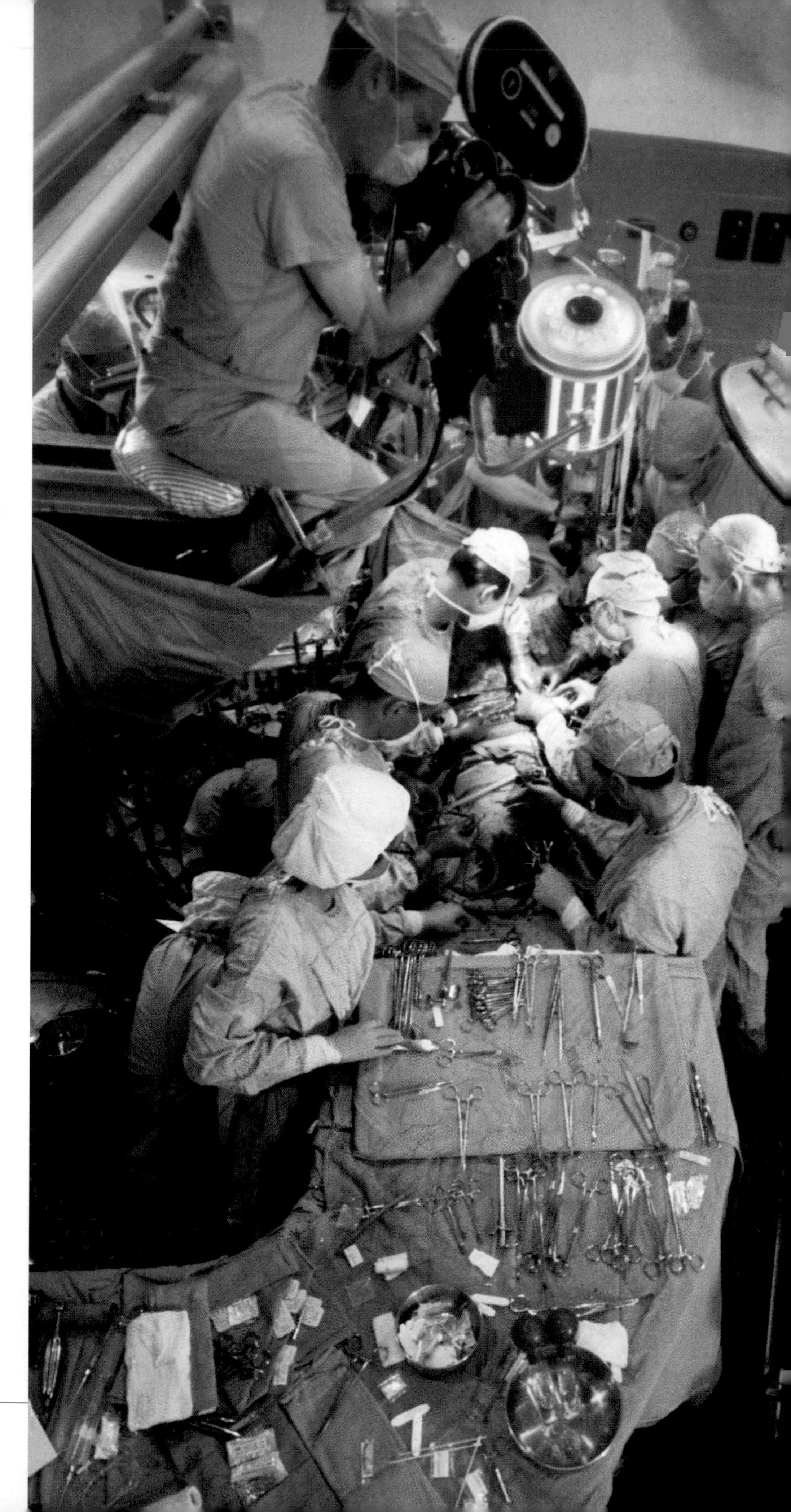

INTO THE HEART Here Dr. Michael DeBakey conducts the third attempt to install an artificial heart pump, 1966

MAGELLANS OF MEDICINE

APRIL 21, 1966: OPERATING TO REPLACE THE HEART For centuries physicians had dreamed of eradicating specific diseases, of replacing injured limbs, arteries and organs, of even transplanting the human heart. But often they found themselves frustrated, stumped by mysteries—like tissue rejection—they didn't understand. In the 20th century many of those riddles were solved through new drugs and surgical techniques, diligent research and advances in technology.

On one front, physicians fought disease through new drugs, beginning with the famously accidental discovery in 1928 of the powerful antibiotic penicillin by a Scot, **Dr. Alexander Fleming.** The crippling polio virus was conquered twice over, for **Dr. Jonas Salk's** 1954 vaccine was eventually replaced by an even easier to use oral vaccine developed by **Dr. Albert Sabin.**

On the surgical front, exciting advances took place in artery, heart and organ replacement. The first consistently successful human grafts, involving the cornea of the eye, were made in 1905. In 1954 **Dr. Joseph E. Murray** transplanted a human kidney, and in the 1950s and 1960s gifted surgeons such as **Dr. Michael DeBakey** made great strides in cardiovascular surgery, leading to the first successful heart-bypass operation in 1967, which routed blood around damaged arteries through healthy vessels grafted from the patient's own body. In December 1967 the world thrilled to the first heart-transplant operation, conducted by **Dr. Christiaan Barnard** in South Africa. Although patient Louis Washkansky died after 18 days of other causes, the road to replacing the human heart was clear. ■

DR. ALEXANDER FLEMING He discovered penicillin in 1928, but it was not widely used until World War II

MY MOTHER, MY SELF

JULY 5, 1996: A CLONED SHEEP IS BORN Roslin, a small village in the green, rolling hills just south of Edinburgh, seems an unlikely locale for a scientific revolution. But it was here that Dr. Ian Wilmut and his colleagues pulled off what many experts thought was a scientific impossibility: from a cell in an adult ewe's mammary gland, they managed to create a frisky lamb named Dolly, scoring an advance in reproductive technology as unsettling as it was startling. Unlike natural offspring, Dolly did not merely take after her biological mother. She was a carbon copy, a laboratory counterfeit so exact that she was in essence her mother's identical twin. Although Wilmut's team struggled for more than 10 years to achieve their goal, it took political and religious leaders around the world no time at all to grasp the import of the event after it was announced in February 1997: if scientists can clone sheep, they can probably clone people too.

The birth of Dolly was the culmination of a biological revolution that began with the work of the 19th century Austrian monk **Gregor Mendel,** whose study of peas pioneered the modern science of genetics. In 1944 **Oswald Avery,** a U.S. bacteriologist, discovered that genetic messages were carried in the nuclei of cells by deoxyribonucleic acid, or DNA. In 1953 Briton **Francis Crick** and American **James Watson** won fame as the first to identify the double-helix structure of DNA. Scientists used this major breakthrough to begin unraveling the genetic code and to diagnose and treat a host of illnesses. Even as Dolly was born, U.S. scientists were far along on the massive **Human Genome Project;** its goal is to locate and identify each gene in man's genetic chain. ■

WATSON AND CRICK They deciphered the double helix

Dolly had survived for seven healthy months before her birth was announced

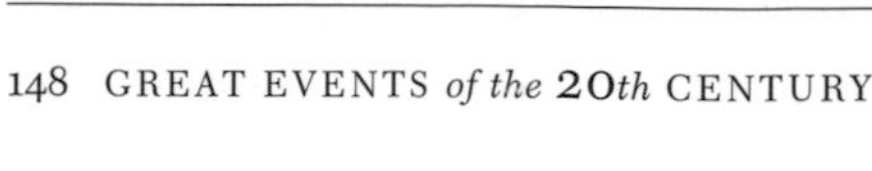

"Today we live in the shadow of AIDS—the terrifyingly modern epidemic that zeroes in on the body's own disease-fighting immune system. More than 15 years after the first rumors of 'gay plague' spread through the bath-

DR. DAVID HO
Man of the Year 1996

houses of New York City and San Francisco, some 30 million people—gays and straights alike—have been infected by HIV, the virus that causes what has been an almost invariably fatal disease. This year, for the first time, there is something ... like hope. Early this summer AIDS patients taking 'cocktails' that combine protease inhibitors with other antiviral drugs began experiencing remarkable recoveries. When the history of this era is written, it is likely that the men and women who turned the tide on AIDS will be seen as true heroes of the age. Dr. David Ho is not a household name. But some people make headlines while others make history."

–TIME, JANUARY 6, 1997

The Babe's Best Season

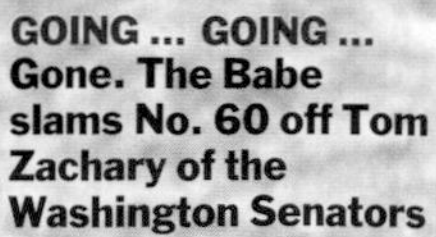

GOING ... GOING ... Gone. The Babe slams No. 60 off Tom Zachary of the Washington Senators

SEPTEMBER 30, 1927 Babe Ruth's big bat—and big heart—put baseball back in the good graces of fans after the 1919 "Black Sox" scandal. The Yankee slugger was unforgettable, even when he struck out, and the times when he did connect were the game's big thrills. Perhaps the biggest was the day in 1927 when Ruth broke his own record for the most home runs in a single season—59, in 1921—by tagging his 60th. By the time Ruth retired in 1935 he had swatted 714 homers. The record —long considered unbreakable—stood until April 8, 1974, when

APRIL 4, 1974 Aaron ties Ruth with No. 714

the Atlanta Braves' Hank Aaron smacked his 715th homer, on his way to a career total of 755. ■

SPORT

Super Bowl III

JANUARY 12, 1969 The first two Super Bowl games between the best teams of the long-established National Football League and the fledgling American Football League had been embarrassing blowouts by the N.F.L. Now here was the cocky Joe Namath, quarterback of the upstart A.F.L.'s cham-

1967 Green Bay's Packers won Super Bowl I

pion New York Jets, "guaranteeing" that his team would whip the Baltimore Colts. Said TIME: "Whatever slim hopes the Jets had of winning centered on Namath's arm—and the only thing he seemed to be exercising was his mouth." But "Broadway Joe" connected on 17 out of 28 passes, and the Jets broke the Colts, 16-7. The biggest winner: professional football, for the Super Bowl had begun to live up to its moniker. ■

ARMED FORCES
Namath's arm—and the Jets' offensive line—whipped the Colts

Rumble in the Jungle

ALI IS GREAT IN EIGHT
With Foreman down in the eighth round, referee Zack Clayton maneuvers Ali to a neutral corner

OCTOBER 30, 1974 Beneath a full moon in Kinshasa, Zaïre, Muhammad Ali stood proud in the ring over the supine form of George Foreman. Ali, 32, had triumphed over a host of opponents: the boxing establishment that had stripped him of his heavyweight title seven years before when Ali had

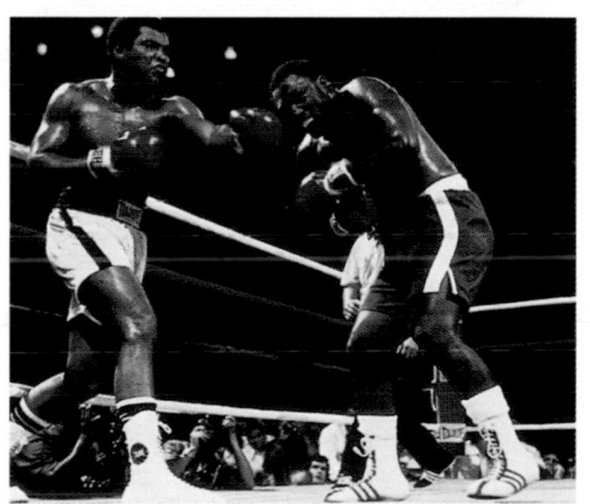

1975 Ali beats a tough Joe Frazier in Manila

refused to be drafted, and the skeptics who rated him a 3-to-1 underdog against the supposedly invincible Foreman, 25. Past his bee-stinging prime, Ali unveiled a new tactic: the rope-a-dope. Through seven rounds he absorbed Foreman's pounding—then he decked his winded foe with a wicked flurry. Said "the Greatest": "The bull is stronger, but the matador is smarter." ■

BLACK GOLD

AUGUST 1936: JESSE OWENS RUIN
HITLER'S OLYMPICS On the first day of competition he brok
the world record for the 100-m dash. On the second day, he won th
final. On the third, he won the broad jump with a new Olymp
record. On the fourth, he won the 200 m—again setting an Olympic record. As a capper, he helped the U.S. 400-m relay team break the world record in winning the event. Yet the victories of black U.S. track star Jesse Owens at the 1936 Berlin Gam were more precious than gold: they repuc ated the racist propaganda of host Ado Hitler, who predicted his Aryan athlet would triumph over "inferior" races.

U.S. AIR POWER
Jesse Owens soars to an Olympic record in the long jump in Berlin

Miles, Milestones and Miracles

ROGER BANNISTER
In May 1954, Briton Roger Bannister smashed a barrier long considered unattainable: he ran the mile in under 4 min., finishing at 3:59.4

MARTINA NAVRATILOVA
In 1990 the Czech-born U.S. star powered her way to a record ninth singles title at Wimbledon, the holiest shrine of tennis

BOBBY JONES
In 1930—as an amateur—he achieved a feat the greatest golfers have never equaled: winning the Grand Slam of the game's four most prestigious tournaments

MICHAEL JORDAN
Twice he led the United States to Olympic gold, and his Chicago Bulls won five N.B.A. titles in the '90s

NADIA COMANECI
At 14, the Romanian gymnast thrilled the world when she scored perfect 10s—the first in modern Olympic history—seven times at the Montreal Games in 1976

20th century

"Notables for miles around had gathered to see Charles S. Chaplin's new picture, *The Gold Rush* ... an epic in comedy, written, acted directed by a man who understands that the cinema is a medium of high art only because it can be used, as can no other medium, to express the illimitable diversity of life."

–TIME, JULY 6, 1925

THE ARTS

ONE GOAL OF THE 20TH CENTURY ARTIST was best expressed by Pablo Picasso's collaborator in the creation of Cubism, Georges Braque. "Art," he said, "is meant to disturb." In the search to question, to provoke, to transgress, the arts became a forum for revolt and a sanctuary for iconoclasts. But Braque got it right: after 90 years, Picasso's *Les Demoiselles d'Avignon* retained the impact TIME art critic Robert Hughes once called "the shock of the new." In the quest to break through, artists found an ally in science. From the Bauhaus school's "machines for living" to a rocker's electric guitar, technology became the secret muse of the time. Indeed, the signature art form of the century—the cinema—wasn't patented by Charlie Chaplin, but by Thomas Edison.

LOUIS ARMSTRONG
FEBRUARY 21, 1949

PABLO PICASSO
JUNE 26, 1950

MIKHAIL BARYSHNIKOV
MAY 19, 1975

"Andy Warhol was a living transparency, with his face pressed to the shop window of the American Dream and his head full of schemes to titillate an aging, youth-obsessed American culture. His contribution to the Pop movement in the early '60s was the image taken from advertising or tabloid journalism: grainy, immediate, a slice of unexplained life registered over and over ... Marilyn Monroe repeated 50 times, 200 Campbell's soup cans, a canvas filled with dollar bills. Absurd though these pictures looked at first, Warhol's fixation on repetition and glut was the most powerful statement ever

ANDY WARHOL
The art of consumption

made by an American artist on the subject of a consumer economy."

—TIME, MARCH 9, 1987

TOWARD CUBISM Working with fellow artist Georges Braque, Picasso would refine the angular planes of *Les*

Demoiselles to create the Cubist style

REALITY REMADE

SPRING 1907: PICASSO PAINTS *LES DEMOISELLES* With a fine sense of historical timing, the young man who would create a new art for the new century, Pablo Picasso, left Barcelona for Paris late in the year 1900. Already a gifted technician, the 19-year-old Spaniard came to Paris seeking inspiration—and liberation from the prevailing academic theories of art. During his early years in Paris he ran through a series of styles; by age 25 he was an able and talented artist, but he was not yet a modern one.

Picasso finally broke through in 1907 with *Les Demoiselles d'Avignon,* which TIME art critic Robert Hughes termed "one of the most astounding feats of ideation in the history of art." Said Hughes: "These days the word radical is patched onto any newish artistic gesture ... this use of the word cannot begin to convey the newness of *Les Demoiselles.* No painting has ever looked more convulsive and contradictory. The sheer intensity of its making is beyond analysis."

The monumental work is a highly stylized depiction of five angular, nude or partially draped women (Avignon was a street of brothels in Barcelona). It was innovative in both its feeling and its form: ruthless in its capturing of aggression (from the painter to his subjects and from the subjects to the viewer) and formally liberating in its exploration of multiple spatial relationships, a process that would lead Picasso to Cubism. Much later, this new combination of pictorial abstraction and personal expression strongly informed the **Abstract Expressionism** of **Jackson Pollock, Willem DeKooning** and other painters of the New York School. ■

1950 Jackson Pollock's subject was the act of painting

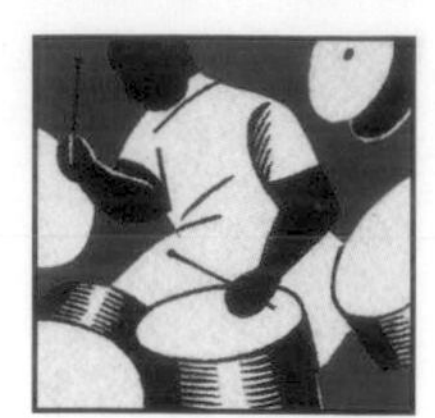

MACHINES FOR LIVING

APRIL 1919: BIRTH OF THE BAUHAUS

Founded by German architect Walter Gropius, the Bauhaus was probably the most stimulating and revolutionary design school of all time. Here artists Paul Klee and Wassily Kandinsky taught alongside architects Marcel Breuer and Ludwig Miës van der Rohe, among others, bringing together all the arts: weaving and furniture making as well as graphics and architecture. Their work, regardless of medium, material or size, recognized the force of industrialism and the beauty of the machine. It was an entirely new way of looking at the world. From the Bauhaus drawing boards, lean, well-proportioned buildings came forth to challenge the neoclassic and Gothic structures of the day.

RAYMOND LOEWY His designs mirrored the century's urgent pace

One of the best examples of the austere new look was Gropius' design for the Bauhaus' new home after the school moved from Weimar to Dessau. Flat-topped and structurally spare, the "machine for living" had horizontal bands of windows that made it seem to hover above the ground rather than rest upon it. This coolly logical modernist form, transcending national influences, came to be known as the International Style.

Influential industrial designers such as America's **Raymond Loewy** would adapt the essentials of their streamlined style from the Bauhaus. But in its belief in architecture as a collaborative process, the Bauhaus was at odds with American master **Frank Lloyd Wright,** who championed the vision of the architect as solitary genius. ■

BACK TO BASICS Radically simple, Gropius' school was a box of glass and concrete

“There is hardly a modern house in the U.S. that does not owe at least some of its features to Frank Lloyd Wright. Among his innovations: the split-level living room, the open plan for house interiors, the corner picture window, the carport (he coined the name too). Wright vociferously maintained his claim to originating modern architecture. But when it came back to him from Europe in the forceful form of works by Gropius, Miës van der Rohe and Le Corbusier, he belabored these men as 'glassic architects' and worse. He dramatically ranged himself against the sweeping tide of the International Style. New York City's United Nations headquarters was a 'tombstone,' Lever House 'a waste of

FRANK LLOYD WRIGHT
A lone, yeasty genius

space,' the Seagram Building 'a whisky bottle on a card table.' Boxy modern houses he called 'coffins for living.'”

–TIME, APRIL 20, 1959

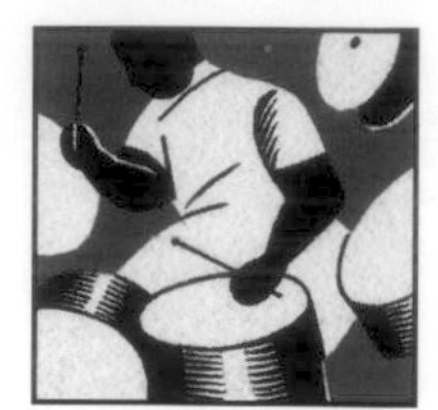

STAGE CENTER

DECEMBER 3, 1947: *A STREETCAR NAMED DESIRE* OPENS Hailing the premiere of Tennessee Williams' second masterpiece in only two years, TIME said, "*A Streetcar Named Desire*...is a fresh, vivid drama, revealing that the author of *The Glass Menagerie* is not only much more of a poet than most of his fellow playwrights, but much more of a realist as well." Poetry and realism: in the tension between them, 20th century theater—under assault from the visual spectacle and close-up techniques of the cinema—took its cue. Samuel Beckett's *Waiting for Godot*, the signature play of the century, captured the tone perfectly.

In performance, British acting greats such as Laurence Olivier and John Gielgud relied on well-honed technical skills, while American actors emulated Marlon Brando—*Streetcar's* steamy Stanley Kowalski—in favoring the more inward, psychologically driven approach of Method acting. Musical theater thrived over the decades: both powerful, as in the great *The Threepenny Opera* of Germans Bertolt Brecht and Kurt Weill, and frivolous, as in the production-heavy extravaganzas of Andrew Lloyd Webber. ■

POWER TRIO
From left, Marlon Brando as Stanley, Kim Hunter as Stella and Jessica Tandy as Blanche in *Streetcar*

Milestones of the Stage

1929: *SHOWBOAT*
This breakthrough work, which turned America's racial divisions into compelling popular art, was based on an Edna Ferber novel of life on a showboat on the Mississippi (the *Ol' Man River* of its most famous song).

1943: *OKLAHOMA!*
Simple on the surface but complex in its integration of dance, character and story, *Oklahoma!* was the first of five hit musicals by the team of Rodgers and Hammerstein.

1949: *DEATH OF A SALESMAN*
Lee J. Cobb, center, starred as the exasperating, self-deluded yet finally sympathetic salesman Willy Loman in Arthur Miller's harrowing story of the American Dream gone wrong.

1956: *WAITING FOR GODOT*
Bert Lahr and E.G. Marshall flopped in the U.S. debut of Samuel Beckett's haunting, stripped-down story of two tramps waiting for a savior who never arrives. *Godot* is now considered a classic.

1981: *CATS*
British composer Andrew Lloyd Webber turned out a sheaf of popular musical spectaculars late in the century. *Cats,* right, and 1986's *The Phantom of the Opera* were long-running international hits.

BIRTH OF A MEDIUM

MARCH 3, 1915: *THE BIRTH OF A NATION* OPENS The movies grew up with the century. In the 1890s the first crude films appeared in France and America; in 1903 the Edison Co. released the first truly commercial movie, *The Great Train Robbery;* in 1913 Cecil B. DeMille shot the first feature film to be made in Hollywood, *The Squaw Man.* But it was in 1915, with the release of **D.W. Griffith's** Civil War epic *The Birth of a Nation,* that the movies began to come into their own as an art form. "As a director," said TIME, "Griffith hit the picture business like a tornado. Before he walked on the set, motion pictures had been static. Griffith rammed his camera into the middle of the action, picking off shots; then he built the shots into sequences, and the sequences into tense, swift narrative. For the first time the movies had a man who realized that while a theater audience listened, a movie audience watched." In the words of his great star **Lillian Gish,** Griffith "gave us the grammar of filmmaking."

1903 *The Great Train Robbery* was the first western

Made on an unparalleled budget ($110,000) and running to an unparalleled length (three hours), *The Birth of a Nation* was the cinema's first "colossal." But it was Griffith's use of such new techniques as the close-up, the long shot in panorama, the fade-in and fade-out, as well as his mastery of the cross-cutting style he had pioneered that established the film as a primer for all future directors—despite its offensive racial stereotypes and its glorification of the Ku Klux Klan. Said French director **René Clair:** "Nothing essential has been added to the art of the motion picture since Griffith." ■

FIND THE HEROES Griffith, who was born in Kentucky, sympathized with the Ku Klux Klan

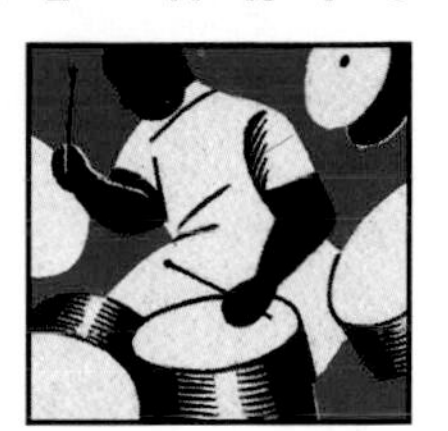

STARDUST

JANUARY 1939: HOLLYWOOD'S GOLDEN YEAR The dark days seemed to have ended at last—the years of the Depression and the dust bowl—and Americans were regaining their pride and self-confidence. The nation's buoyant mood was reflected in its movies: 1939 was the greatest year of Hollywood's Golden Age.

There was **Gone With the Wind,** whose production attracted more intense public curiosity than any other film ever made. But producer David O. Selznick's Civil War epic was just one in the astonishing list of great films released in 1939. There was also **The Wizard of Oz,** the grandest and most glorious of all fantasies, and **Stagecoach,** the model for all westerns to come. Then there was the dark gothic romance of **Wuthering Heights;** adventure stories like *Beau Geste* and *Drums Along the Mohawk;* sophisticated comedies like *Ninotchka* and *The Women.* Tearjerkers? How about *Intermezzo* or *Goodbye, Mr. Chips*? Politics? Try Frank Capra's populist parable *Mr. Smith Goes to Washington.*

Everyone worked hard in the fantasy factories of 1939. Jimmy Stewart's fans had five movies to choose from, and so did Henry Fonda's. Behind the cameras were directors whose best work is now avidly studied in film schools: **John Ford, George Cukor, Cecil B. DeMille** and **William Wyler.** Behind them were such all-powerful producers as **Louis B. Mayer, Darryl F. Zanuck** and the brothers Warner. And behind it all was a huge audience: 85 million people—a figure equal to two-thirds of the U.S. population—went to the movies each week. Never again would Hollywood have the brash confidence of that year of genius and glitter. ■

NOT KANSAS ***The Wizard of Oz*** **is Hollywood's best fantasy**

BLOCKBUSTER ***Gone With the Wind*** **earned a record $32 million at the box office by 1943**

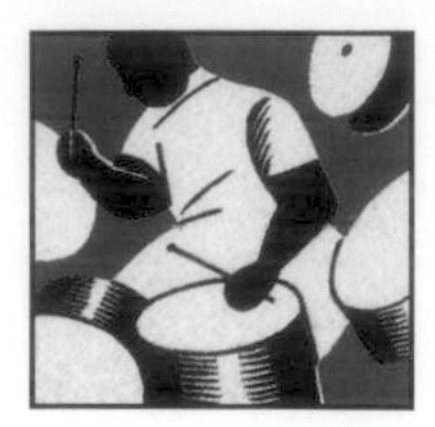

SCREEN RITES

MODERN SAVAGES
Apocalypse Now* related the barbarity of Vietnam to the Congo of Conrad's 1902 novella *Heart of Darkness

AUGUST 15, 1979: *APOCALYPSE NOW* OPENS

Like D.W. Griffith's *The Birth of a Nation* and Victor Fleming's *Gone With the Wind,* Francis Ford Coppola's *Apocalypse Now* dug deep into a defining American conflict to create a masterpiece. Based on Joseph Conrad's 1902 novella *Heart of Darkness,* the movie framed the surreal Vietnam War against larger issues—power, colonialism and empire—that shaped the century.

With the fade-out of cinema empires—the great studios that had given Hollywood its Golden Age—creative power in American films passed from the old, omnipotent studio moguls to a new phalanx of visionary directors: Coppola, Robert Altman and George Lucas, among many others. Yet most U.S. films remained driven by box-office concerns, while directors elsewhere—such as Ingmar Bergman, François Truffaut, Federico Fellini and Akira Kurosawa—explored film as an art form. By the 1990s Hollywood was in a rut, producing ever more costly blockbusters to attract the widest possible audience, at the expense of artistic vision. Its movies had never been more profitable—or less meaningful. ■

Great Directors, Milestone Movies

ORSON WELLES
***Citizen Kane* (1941), near right, often cited as the greatest American film, is a study of power and corruption based on the life of W.R. Hearst.**

INGMAR BERGMAN
***The Seventh Seal* (1957), far right, a fable of medieval life during the plague, typifies the often bleak, probing works of the Swede, who was also a gifted theater director.**

AKIRA KUROSAWA
***Rashomon* (1950) tells the tale of a brutal murder from four points of view, posing paradoxical questions about the nature of truth in highly dramatic form. Kurosawa's elegant meditations on violence inspired imitators: *The Seven Samurai* became *The Magnificent Seven; Yojimbo* became *A Fistful of Dollars,* which was among the early Clint Eastwood spaghetti westerns.**

FEDERICO FELLINI
***La Dolce Vita* (1960) was one of a string of masterpieces turned out by the prodigal Italian master of fantasy. His major films include *8½, Juliet of the Spirits* and *Amarcord*. Exuberant and even overdone, erotic and playful, Fellini movies were celluloid circuses brimming with the director's infatuation with the hurly-burly of the big top.**

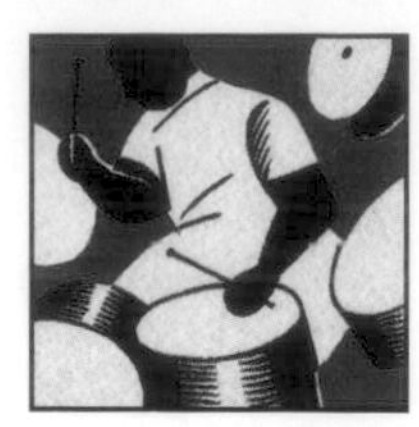

STEP BY STEP

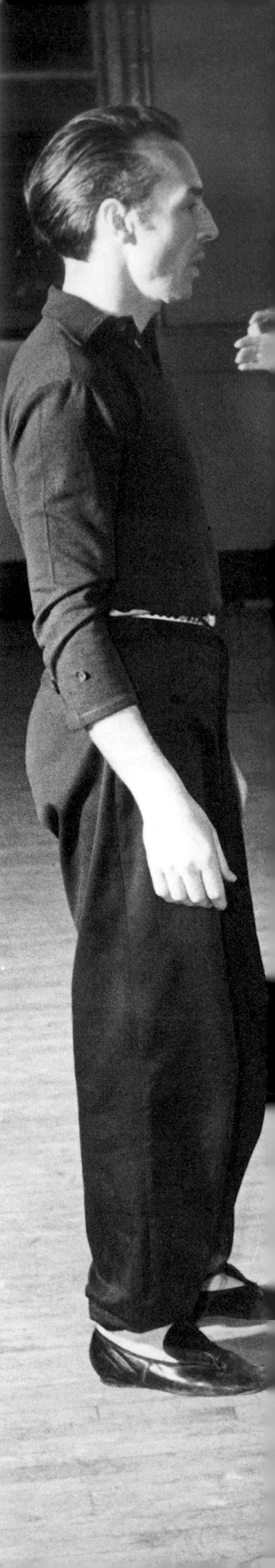

JANUARY 1, 1934: THE SCHOOL OF AMERICAN BALLET OPENS The time was wrong: it was the middle of the Depression. The country was wrong: America had no tradition of classical dance. But the two men who started the new ballet academy were exactly right. The visionary and financial force behind the enterprise was Lincoln Kirstein, a 27-year-old arts lover from a wealthy Boston family. The chairman of the faculty (which numbered three, including himself), was the 30-year-old former chief choreographer of impresario **Serge Diaghilev's** legendary Ballet Russes, George Balanchine.

Kirstein had lured Balanchine to the New World with the grandest of visions: to create a tradition of classical dance in the U.S. The two farsighted men agreed that the proper foundation for such a lofty plan was not a ballet company but a school that would train the dancers necessary for the evolution of a company.

1935: Martha Graham's powerful *Primitive Mysteries* debuted

The plan succeeded, brilliantly. The School of American Ballet laid the groundwork for the New York City Ballet; from its debut in 1948, the NYCB became the showcase for Balanchine's world-conquering neoclassical style.

The U.S. was also the home of the second innovative force in 20th century dance, the modern style pioneered by **Ruth St. Denis,** her husband **Ted Shawn** and by **Martha Graham.** Always seeking fresh forms to capture the tempo of the times, they rejected the traditional postures of classical ballet to create expressive new vocabularies of movement. The two schools propelled dance to new popularity and prominence among the century's arts. ■

STARTING SMALL
In the 1930s few Americans had even seen classical ballet

"The dancer is short, with rounded muscles and the pale face of a man made up permanently as Petrouchka. Yet when he launches his perfectly arched body into the arc of one of his improbably sustained leaps—high, light, the leg beats blurring precision—he transcends the limits of physique and, it seems, those of gravity itself. He is an unbelievable technician with invisible technique. If one goes by the gasps in the theater or the ecstasies of the critics, such

MIKHAIL BARYSHNIKOV
Defected to the U.S. in 1974

moments turn Mikhail Baryshnikov, if not into a minor god, then into a major sorcerer. It is less than a year since he defected from a Soviet touring company in Toronto, but the public has made him a superstar and calls him by his nickname: 'Misha.' "

—TIME, MAY 19, 1975

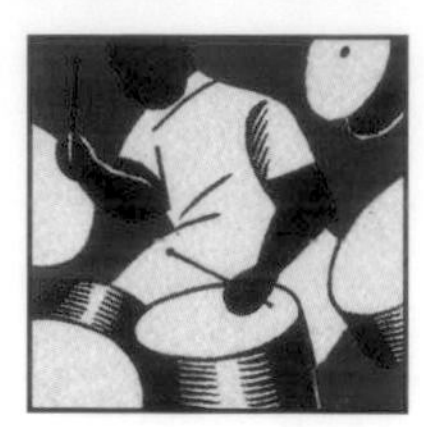

ESCAPE ARTIST

OCTOBER 1904: THE EXILE OF JAMES JOYCE

Oppressed by his native land ("the old sow that eats her farrow"), James Joyce left Ireland at age 22 to spend his most creative years abroad. His intention, he said, was to live in "silence, exile and cunning." In the autobiographical novel the gifted rebel began in that seminal year, *A Portrait of the Artist as a Young Man,* he grandly proclaimed a far loftier goal: "To forge in the smithy of my soul the uncreated conscience of my race."

YANKEE EXILE Poet T.S. Eliot left the U.S. for Britain

Joyce succeeded brilliantly with his masterpiece, *Ulysses,* whose action is set in a single day: June 16, 1904. But as TIME noted in 1934, "The wanderings of *Ulysses* have been longer if less arduous than those of its namesake." Joyce finished his seventh year of writing on the novel in 1921; installments were printed in the literary journal *Little Review,* but the U.S. Postal Service seized copies of the magazine for obscenity. An American book lover, Sylvia Beach, sponsored a small printing of the book in France and presented the first edition to Joyce on his 40th birthday in 1922. *Ulysses* was banned in America until a ruling by Federal Judge John M. Woolsey in 1933 allowed Random House to publish a U.S. edition.

Joyce's exile prefigured the involuntary cultural dislocation of many major 20th century writers. **Thomas Mann** fled Hitler's Germany; **Aleksandr Solzhenitsyn** was a prisoner in the Soviet Gulag; in the 1990s **Salman Rushdie** lived underground, fugitive from a 1989 Islamic *fatwa,* or death sentence, for his allegedly blasphemous novel *The Satanic Verses.* ■

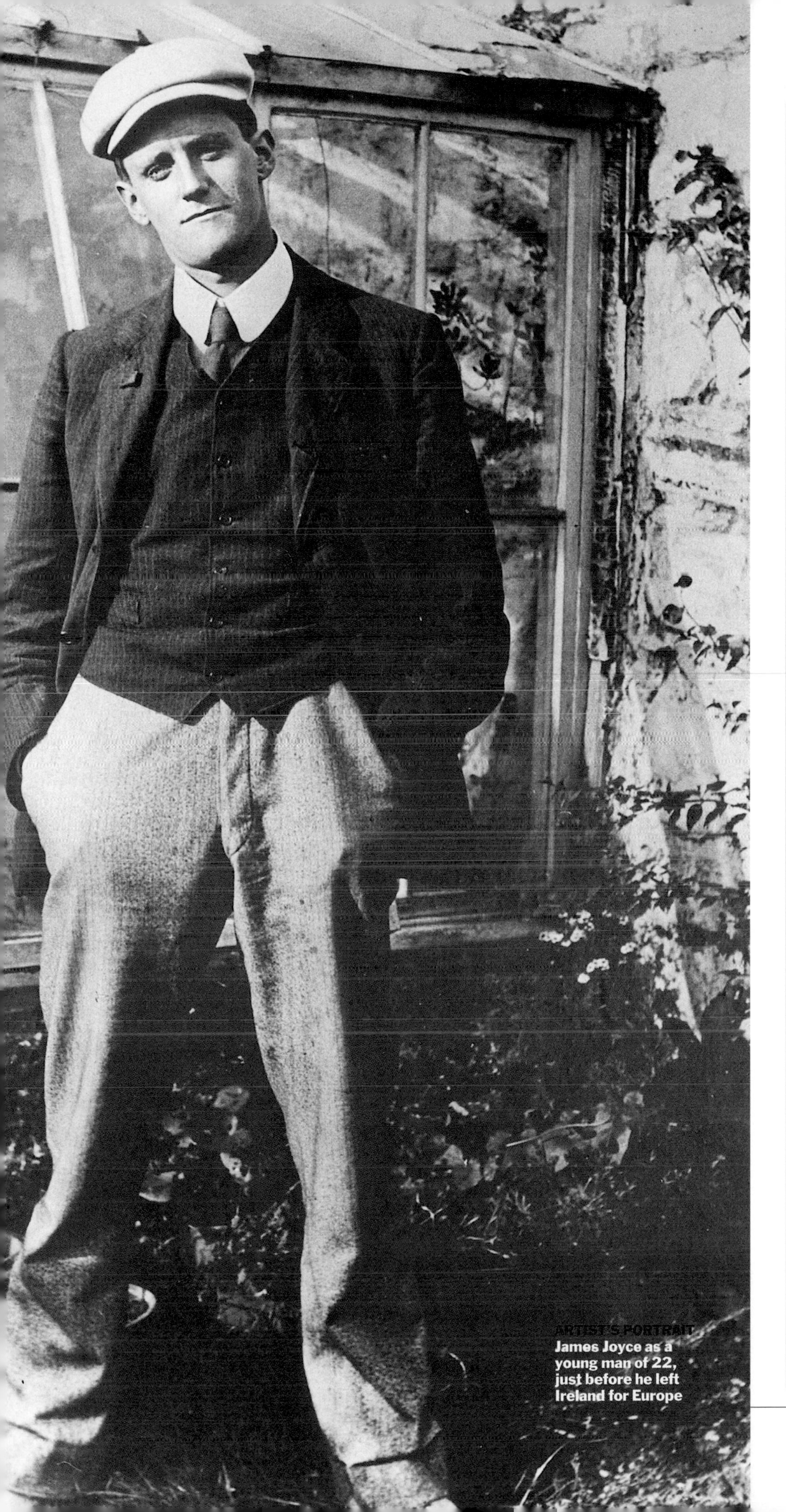

ARTIST'S PORTRAIT James Joyce as a young man of 22, just before he left Ireland for Europe

Dread and Magic

FRANZ KAFKA
Prophet of paranoia

While the elaborate wordplay and formal inventiveness of James Joyce were echoed in the work of such novelists as France's Marcel Proust and America's William Faulkner, other literary schools flourished. In Eastern Europe a darkly enigmatic style, pioneered by Austrian writer Franz Kafka in such works as

GABRIEL GARCIA MARQUEZ
Master of magic realism

The Metamorphosis (1915), expressed the claustrophobia and paranoia of the region's politics. In Latin America fiction blossomed into a flamboyant, surrealistic form. Magic realism, which suffused everyday life with evanescent fantasies, came of age in 1967 in Colombian writer Gabriel García Márquez's *100 Years of Solitude*.

Russian School

The Conservatory in St. Petersburg, Russia, was the great hothouse for serious music in the 20th century. Among its students:

SERGEI RACHMANINOV
His lyricism won applause

the brilliant pianist Sergei Rachmaninov, whose works in the Russian romantic tradition—such as *Rhapsody on a Theme of Paganini* (1934)—achieved broad popularity. A sadder fate befell Dmitri Shostakovich, a gifted, prolific composer who had the misfortune to live under Stalinism; his more adventurous work was criticized

DMITRI SHOSTAKOVICH
His modernism riled Stalin

for failing to meet the optimistic standards of the Soviet state. A third Conservatory student, Sergei Prokofiev, was hailed for such works as *Peter and the Wolf* (1936) but was also criticized for his "formalist tendencies."

SPRING FEVER

MAY 29, 1913: *THE RITE OF SPRING* PREMIERES He was the son of a famed Russian singer and an orchestration student of Rimsky-Korsakov's. But Igor Stravinsky was more interested in the future than the past. His destination: a new musical idiom that would shatter old clichés. His ticket: a work of thrilling modernity, *The Rite of Spring.* Following two successful, somewhat innovative ballet scores, *The Firebird* (1910) and *Petrouchka* (1911), Stravinsky shocked Paris with his new work, a sophisticated evocation of primitive myths and energies that roiled with unprecedented rhythmic power.

Conductor Pierre Monteux recalled that when he first heard Stravinsky run through *The Rite* on the piano, bobbing up and down to accentuate its jagged rhythms, "I was convinced that he was raving mad." Later, when the work had its premiere at the Théâtre des Champs Elysées, many members of the audience thought so too. They erupted in perhaps the most notorious riot in music history: they booed, they fought with one another, they even pelted Monteux and the players with programs and hats.

Polytonal, polymodal, polyrhythmic, *The Rite* did not so much reject conventional harmony as it brought contrasting tonalities crashing dangerously together, jarring the 20th century out of its lingering romanticism and announcing a new consciousness. Composer Pierre Boulez called *The Rite* "the cornerstone of modern music," for it influenced Stravinsky's fellow Russians **Sergei Prokofiev** and **Dmitri Shostakovich,** as well as the Americans **Aaron Copland, George Gershwin** and **Samuel Barber.** ■

1935 The debut of George Gershwin's *Porgy and Bess*

REBEL OR DANDY? **Stravinsky was 32 in 1913, and looking sharp in a Paris flat**

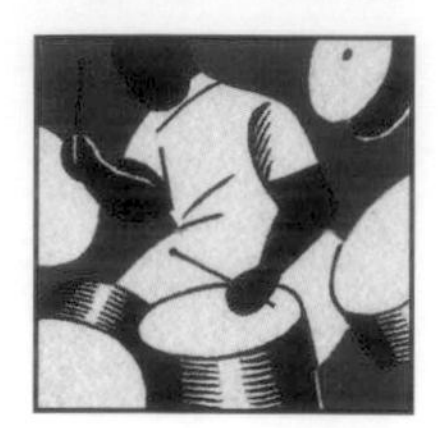

ALL THAT JAZZ

JULY 7, 1956: DUKE ELLINGTON AT NEWPORT The greatest jazz solo of the century? It might seem an impossible task to identify a single transcendent moment in a form devoted to exuberant improvisation. But many jazz fans would settle on the last night of the Newport Jazz Festival of 1956, when the big band led by Duke Ellington ripped into the composer's 1937 classic, *Diminuendo and Crescendo in Blue,* with tenor saxophonist Paul Gonsalves soloing through an incredible 27 choruses. Five weeks later, Ellington was on the cover of TIME, which reported, "The event confirmed a turning point in a career... the Ellington band was once again the most exciting thing in the business... the composer's style contains the succinctness of concert music and the excitement of jazz."

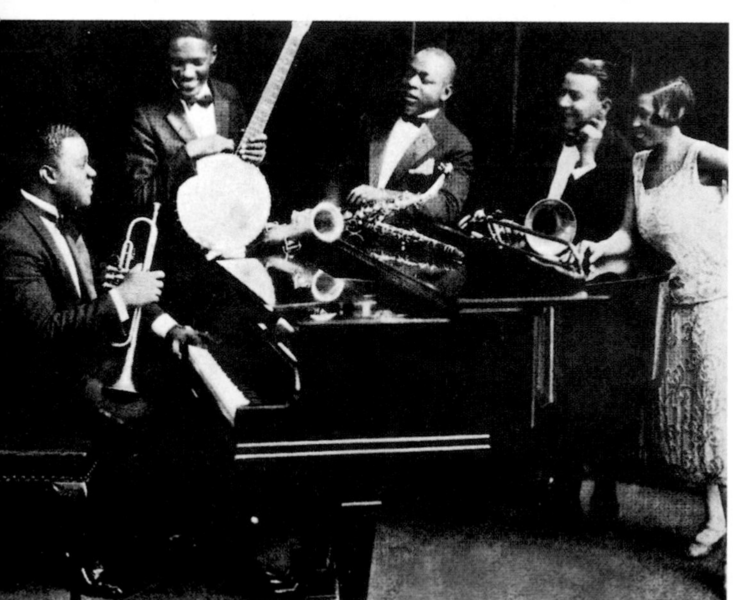

HOT FIVE Louis Armstrong, left, led the Jazz Age's best combo

Often cited as America's only indigenous art form, jazz emerged from black New Orleans in the first decades of the century—right alongside its greatest early exponent, **Louis Armstrong,** whose Hot Five combo of the 1920s turned the music into a national sensation.

Bandleader-clarinetist **Benny Goodman's** 1938 concert at Carnegie Hall served notice that jazz was a serious form. Said TIME: "In the late Mr. Carnegie's polite plaster shrine last Sunday night, at Mr. Goodman's 'jam session,' the audience of 3,000, infected, pounded its feet in unison. In the best and truest sense, the joint actually was rocking." ■

SIR DUKE Leading the band from the piano, Ellington, 57, revitalized his career at Newport

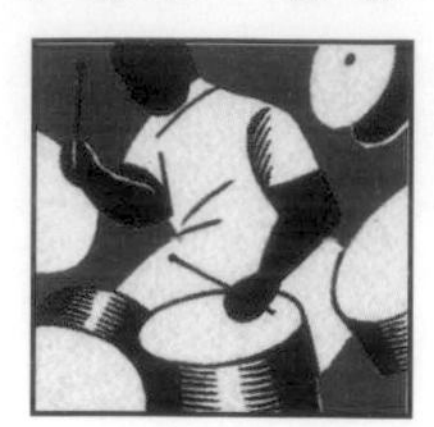

ROCK ROLLS IN

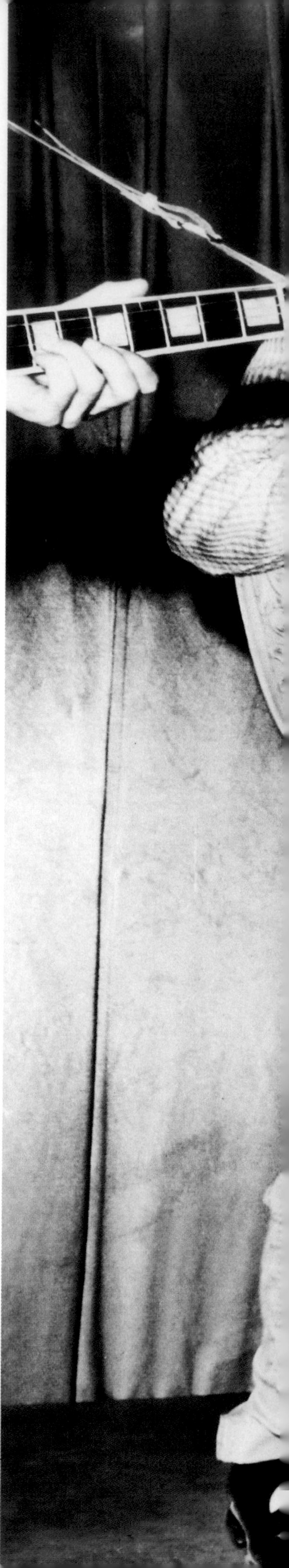

JANUARY 17, 1956: ELVIS PRESLEY'S *HEARTBREAK HOTEL* IS RELEASED He was not, as he has so often been called, "the father of rock 'n' roll," but Elvis Presley was the first to consolidate all its divergent roots into a single, surly, hard-driving style. Rock had its origins deep in rhythm and blues, which, in a time of strict musical segregation, was black music all the way. **Sam Phillips,** the producer who recorded Presley's first great sessions in 1955 at the Sun Records studios in Memphis, freely admitted that he had been looking for a "black sound inside a white boy." He found his man—or boy—in the young Elvis. To the rollicking rock of **Chuck Berry** and the gritty blues of **Muddy Waters,** Presley brought a gloss of country-and-western and a rockabilly beat. Yet Presley preserved an undertone of sexuality, particularly in his provocative stage gyrations, while accentuating the music's rough edges of danger, from its sharp beat to its streetwise lyrics.

FEBRUARY 1964 Ed Sullivan fosters U.S. Beatlemania

But "The King" lost his fire, and when the talented singer/songwriter **Buddy Holly** was killed in a plane crash, rock languished in its homeland—until February 1964, when a hugely popular British pop group, **the Beatles,** appeared on *The Ed Sullivan Show.* Larky, photogenic—and carefully groomed for success by manager Brian Epstein—the "Fab Four" conquered America with ease.

A final essential influence on the growth of pop music into a legitimate art form came from **Bob Dylan,** the young American singer who combined the social awareness of folk music with the hallucinatory lyricism of the Beat movement. Dylan's evolution from folk poet to angry rocker—sprung full-blown on a hostile audience at the Newport Folk Festival in 1965—divided his fans at the time but forged the future of rock. ■

Presley's sexy moves horrified parents—and thrilled their kids

"There he stands, and who can believe him? Black corduroy cap, green corduroy shirt, blue corduroy pants. Hard-lick guitar, whooping harmonica, beardless chin, skinny little voice that sounds as if it were drifting over the walls of a tuberculosis sanatorium. At 22, he looks 14, and his accent belongs to a jive Nebraskan, or maybe a Brooklyn hillbilly. He is a dime-store philosopher, a drugstore cowboy, a men's room conversationalist. There is something faintly ridiculous about such a citybilly. But he has something unique to say, and he says it in songs of his own invention—as

BOB DYLAN
In Mississippi, 1963

in his finest, *Blowin' in the Wind*—that are the best of their style since Woody Guthrie's."

–TIME, MAY 31, 1963

INDEX

INDEX

CREDITS

Credits read from left to right and from top to bottom of page, except as noted. All TIME covers © Time Inc.

Editorial illustrations by Brian Cronin.

Front cover NASA

Table of contents Wesley Frank/Woodfin Camp

Introduction 2 Archive Photos/Museum of the City of New York **4** Culver Pictures, The Mansell Collection/Time Inc., AP/Wide World **5** Corbis Bettmann, Musee Picasso/Paris, no credit, James Keyser

Nations 8 Brown Brothers **9** UPI/Corbis Bettmann **10** The Mansell Collection/Time Inc. **11** The Mansell Collection/Time Inc. The New York *Times* **12** Karl Knaur **13** U.S. Signal Corps **14** UPI/Corbis Bettmann **15** The Mansell Collection/Time Inc. **16** U.S. Signal Corps **17** U.S. Signal Corp, Brown Brothers **18** Harris & Ewing **19** WPA Picture Records **20** The Mansell Collection/Time Inc. (2) **21** UPI/Corbis Bettmann **22** no credit **23** AP/Wide World (2) **24** Ullstein Bilderdienst **25** AP/Wide World, Dever/Black Star **26** Keystone, Pictures Inc/TIME **27** New York *Times* Paris Bureau Collection/National Archives **28** Ralph Morse/LIFE, U.S. Naval Photographic Center **30** UPI/Corbis Bettmann, U.S. Coast Guard **31** Yevgeny Khaldei **32** Carl Mydans/LIFE **33** Bernard Hoffman/LIFE, Carl Mydans/LIFE **34** Keystone, James Burke/LIFE, John Phillips/LIFE **35** John Phillips/LIFE **36** Hank Walker/LIFE, Walter Sanders/LIFE **38** David Douglas Duncan/LIFE **39** Carl Mydans/LIFE **40** John Sadovy/LIFE **41** Walter Sanders/LIFE, Luis Sanchez **42** Cecil Stoughton/LIFE, ©1997 Abraham Zapruder **43** Bob Jackson/Dallas *Times Herald* **44** Eddie Adams/AP **45** John Olson/LIFE **46** Bill Eppridge/LIFE, Hubert Van Es/UPI/Corbis Bettmann, UPI/Corbis Bettmann **48** Steve Northup/TIME **49** Bill Pierce/TIME, Steve Northup/TIME **50** Raymond Depardon/Gamma Liaison, David DeVoss/TIME, Ted Lau/TIME, David Rubinger/TIME **51** Abbas/Magnum **52** Takayuki Senzaki, Atsuko Otsuka/Photo Shuttle/Japan, (inset) Widener/AP Wide World **53** John Dominis/LIFE **54** James Nachtwey/Black Star, Alain DeJean/Sygma, Laski/Sipa/Black Star **55** Cleaver/Press Association, Terry Ashe/TIME **56** Rudi Frey/TIME, Alexandra Avakian/Woodfin Camp **57** Chip Hires/Gamma Liaison **58** Thomas Hartwell/TIME **59** Sygma **60** Cynthia Johnson/TIME **61** David Rubinger/TIME **62** Louise Gubb/JB Pictures **63** Denis Farrel/AP for TIME **64** (inset) AP Wide World, Lisa Rudy/Black Star **65** Michael Gallacher/Gamma Liaison

Business 68 Pierre Boulat/LIFE, Courtesy Volkswagen **69** Corbis Bettman, Jack Birns **70** Emil J. Kloes/Courtesy Russell Sage Foundation **71** Corbis Bettmann, The Tilly Library/Indiana University, Brown Brothers **72** AP/Wide World **73** UPI/Corbis Bettmann **74** UPI/Corbis Bettmann **75** David Douglas Duncan/LIFE, Clark Misher/Alaska Stock Images **76** Don Uhrbrock, UPI/Corbis Bettmann **77** Courtesy *Justice*/(I.L.G.W.U.) **78** no credit **79** Culver Pictures, CBS **80** IBM, Leo Choplin/TIME **81** no credit **82** no credit **83** David Gahr/TIME, no credit, Henry Groskinsky/LIFE, AP/Wide World **84** AP/Wide World **85** Culver Pictures **87** UPI/Corbis Bettmann, (inset) Brown Brothers **88** Keystone **89** National Archives **91** UPI/Corbis Bettmann **92** Bruce Weaver/AP Wide World

Society 96 Todd Bigelow/Black Star **97** Brown Brothers **98** Owen Franken/Sygma UPI/Corbis Bettmann **99** Jean Pierre Lafont/Sygma **100** UPI/Corbis Bettmann **101** UPI/Corbis Bettmann, AP Wide World **102** AP/Wide World **103** UPI/Corbis Bettmann (2) **104** Charles Moore/Black Star **105** Paul Schutzer/LIFE, UPI/Corbis Bettmann **106** John Malmen **107** Joseph Louw **108** UPI/Corbis Bettmann **109** David Lees/LIFE, Archive Photos **110** Brown Brothers, UPI/Corbis Bettmann **111** Myung J. Chun/Pool, AP/Wide World (2) **112** Nicole Bengiveno/Matrix for TIME, Paul Fusco/Magnum **113** Paul Fusco/Magnum **114** Alfred Eisenstadt/LIFE, Al Grillo/Picture Group **115** David Gahr/TIME

Discoveries 116 Courtesy of Paul Popper, Ltd. **117** Courtesy the National Geographic Society from Tim Gidal **118** Harry Burton/The Metropolitan Museum of Art, (inset) Fred Maroon **120** M. Lariviere/Laval Archives **123** British Mount Everest Expedition/The *Times* of London (2) **124** R. Melloul/Sygma

Science 128 Brown Brothers **129** The Mansell Collection/Time, Inc. Underwood & Underwood **130** Corbis Bettmann, Pix Inc./TIME **132** Boston *Sunday Globe* Rotogravure Section, no credit, Lucent Technologies **134** Chicago *Tribune* **135** AP/Wide World, UPI/Corbis Bettmann **136** AP/Wide World **137** UPI/Corbis Bettmann **138** Smithsonian Institution, AP/Wide World, Sovfoto/Eastfoto, Neil Leifer/TIME **139** Sovfoto/Eastfoto **140** NASA **141** Neil A. Armstrong/NASA **142** NASA **143** NASA **144** Des Bartlett/Armand Denis Productions, National Museum of Ethiopia/Photo ©1985 David L. Brill **145** David L. Brill ©National Geographic Society **146** Werner Wolff/Black Star, Ralph Morse/LIFE **147** Brown Brothers **148** Camera Press/Pix Inc. **149** AP/PA Files, Gregory Heisler/Outline

Sport 150 UPI/Corbis Bettmann **151** Carl Skalag, Jr./SI **152** UPI/Corbis Bettmann **153** Vernon Biever/SI **154** Ken Regan/Camera 5, Neil Leifer/SI, **156** UPI/Corbis Bettmann **157** Oxford *Daily Mail*, D. Walbert/SI, UPI/Corbis Bettmann, Barry Gossage/NBA Photos, Neil Leifer/SI

The Arts 160 Mikel Way/CSU, Museum of Modern Art/Acquired through the Lilly P. Bliss bequest ©1997 Estate of Pablo Picasso/Paris **161** Ralph Burckhardt **162** Ulan Craux/Paris **163** Foto Marburg/Art Resource/NY, ©Karsh/Woodfin Camp **164** Archive Photos/Museum of the City of New York **165** no credit, Gjon Mili/LIFE, W.E. Smith/LIFE, Eliot Erwitt/LIFE, Gregory Heisler/Outline/*Cats* **166** George Eastman House **167** Culver Pictures **168** Courtesy Museum of Modern Art/Film Stills Archive, no credit **170** Kobal Collection **171** RKO Radio Pix, Photofest, RKO Radio Pix, Gianni Pratarlon/Pierluigi **172** ©Barbara Morgan/Willard & Barbara Morgan/Time Inc. licensee **173** Pix Inc./Time Inc., Jack Vartoogian **174** Pictorial Parade **175** C.P. Curran, no credit, AP Wide World **176** AP Wide World, Sovfoto **177** no credit, Vandamm Studio **178** Bill Spilka/Archive Photos **179** Jack Bradley **180** Bill Eppridge/LIFE **181** Frank Driggs/Magnum, Danny Lyon/Magnum

Back cover Carl Mydans/LIFE, Library of Congress, Alexandria Avakian/Woodfin Camp, Bill Eppridge/TIME, AP Wide World